A Guide to Working with Visual Logic

Thad Crews and Chip Murphy

COURSE TECHNOLOGY
CENGAGE Learning

Australia • Brazil • Japan • Korea • Mexico • Singapore • Spain • United Kingdom • United States

COURSE TECHNOLOGY
CENGAGE Learning

A Guide to Working with Visual Logic
Thad Crews and Chip Murphy

Executive Editor: Marie Lee

Acquisitions Editor: Amy Jollymore

Managing Editor: Tricia Coia

Editorial Assistant: Patrick Frank

Marketing Manager: Bryant Chrzan

Senior Content Project Manager: Jill Braiewa

Art Director: Marissa Falco

Print Buyer: Julio Esperas

Production Service: International Typesetting and Composition

Proofreader: Green Pen Quality Assurance

Indexer: Alexandra Nickerson

Quality Assurance: Chris Scriver, Danielle Shaw

Cover Designer: Cabbage Design

Cover Photos:
  Main: Photodisc/Veer/Getty Images
  Inset: ©iStockphoto.com/Hshen Lim

Compositor: International Typesetting and Composition

For product information and technology assistance, contact us at
Cengage Learning Customer & Sales Support, 1-800-354-9706

For permission to use material from this text or product,
submit all requests online at **cengage.com/permissions**
Further permissions questions can be e-mailed to
permissionrequest@cengage.com

ISBN-13: 978-0-324-60119-0

ISBN-10: 0-324-60119-0

Course Technology
25 Thomson Place
Boston, MA 02210
USA

Cengage Learning is a leading provider of customized learning solutions with office locations around the globe, including Singapore, the United Kingdom, Australia, Mexico, Brazil, and Japan. Locate your local office at: **international.cengage.com/region**

Cengage Learning products are represented in Canada by Nelson Education, Ltd.

For your lifelong learning solutions, visit **course.cengage.com**

Purchase any of our products at your local college store or at our preferred online store **www.ichapters.com**

Printed in the United States of America
4 5 6 7 14 13 12

BRIEF CONTENTS

PREFACE   IX

CHAPTER 1 INPUT, PROCESS, OUTPUT   1

CHAPTER 2 MAKING DECISIONS   19

CHAPTER 3 WHILE LOOPS   37

CHAPTER 4 FOR LOOPS AND NESTED LOOPS   59

CHAPTER 5 ARRAYS   73

CHAPTER 6 GRAPHICS AND PROCEDURES   97

APPENDIX A VISUAL LOGIC RESERVED WORDS   125

APPENDIX B DEBUGGING IN VISUAL LOGIC   126

APPENDIX C USING MULTIMEDIA   129

INDEX   130

TABLE OF CONTENTS

PREFACE   IX

CHAPTER 1 INPUT, PROCESS, OUTPUT   1

INTRODUCTION   1

LOGIC AND SYNTAX   2

YOUR FIRST PROGRAM: HELLO WORLD   3

YOUR SECOND PROGRAM: HELLO NAME   5

   Simple Programming Formats   6

WEEKLY PAYCHECK PROGRAM   7

   Step 1: Input   7

   Step 2: Processing   8

   Step 3: Output   9

HOW TO WRITE ARITHMETIC EXPRESSIONS   11

QUICK CHECK 1-A   12

QUICK CHECK 1-B   12

   Strategies for Doing Conversions   12

INTRINSIC FUNCTIONS   13

DEBUGGING WITH VISUAL LOGIC   14

CHAPTER SUMMARY   16

   Key Terms   16

   Review Questions   16

   Programming Exercises   16

CHAPTER 2 MAKING DECISIONS   19

MAKING DECISIONS   19

THE IF STATEMENT   20

QUICK CHECK 2-A   21

   Simple IF Statements   21

   Solving the Overtime Problem   22

NESTED IF STATEMENTS   23

   Long-Distance Billing Problem   24

COMPOUND CONDITIONS   25

QUICK CHECK 2-B   27

CHAPTER SUMMARY   33

   Key Terms   33

   Review Questions   33

   Programming Exercises   33

CHAPTER 3 WHILE LOOPS   37

CONSOLE INPUT AND OUTPUT   37
  Console End-of-Output Character   38
WHILE LOOPS   40
QUICK CHECK 3-A   45
WHILE LOOPS AND SENTINEL VALUES   46
EXIT LOOP   49
CHAPTER SUMMARY   53
  Key Terms   53
  Review Questions   53
  Programming Exercises   54

CHAPTER 4 FOR LOOPS AND NESTED LOOPS   59

FOR LOOPS   59
  Comparing While Loops and For Loops   60
  Working with Final and Step Values   61
NESTED LOOPS   63
CHAPTER SUMMARY   69
  Key Terms   69
  Review Questions   69
  Programming Exercises   69

CHAPTER 5 ARRAYS   73

ARRAYS   74
  Creating an Array   74
  Accessing Individual Elements of an Array   74
BENEFITS OF USING AN ARRAY   75
SAMPLE PROGRAM #1: EVENS AND ODDS   78
  Analysis and Design   79
SAMPLE PROGRAM #2: DICE ROLL SIMULATION   81
  Analysis and Design   81
SAMPLE PROGRAM #3: PARALLEL ARRAYS (USERNAME AND PASSWORD)   83
  Reading Data from a Text File   83
  Analysis and Design   84
CHAPTER SUMMARY   91
  Key Terms   91
  Review Questions   91
  Programming Exercises   91

CHAPTER 6 GRAPHICS AND PROCEDURES   97

GRAPHICS   98
  Forward and Turn Right   98
QUICK CHECK 6-A   101
  Using Loops   102

WORKING WITH COLORS   103
   Set Color and Pen Width   104
   Color Forward   105
QUICK CHECK 6-B   105
STRUCTURED DESIGN USING PROCEDURES   106
   Rotating Flags Problem   106
   Creating a Procedure   107
QUICK CHECK 6-C   110
PROCEDURES WITH PARAMETERS   110
   Rotating Shapes Program   110
   Visual Logic Implementation   111
RECURSION   114
CHAPTER SUMMARY   121
   Key Terms   121
   Review Questions   121
   Programming Exercises   121

APPENDIX A   VISUAL LOGIC RESERVED WORDS   **125**

APPENDIX B   DEBUGGING IN VISUAL LOGIC   **126**
COMMON MISTAKE #1: CHECK FOR MISSPELLED VARIABLE NAMES   126
COMMON MISTAKE #2: MULTIPLE VARIABLE NAMES   127
DEBUGGING–PENCIL AND PAPER   127
DEBUGGING–BREAKPOINTS AND VARIABLE WATCH   127

APPENDIX C   USING MULTIMEDIA   **129**

INDEX   **130**

PREFACE

A Guide to Working with Visual Logic is the perfect companion for use with the software package "Visual Logic," a tool that combines the graphics of flowcharts (visual representations of algorithms) and the utility of pseudo-code (a minimal syntax description of an algorithm) into a single simulation tool. In combination with the software, *A Guide to Working with Visual Logic* will provide novice programming students with a minimal-syntax introduction to essential programming concepts including variables, input, assignment, output, conditions, loops, procedures, arrays, and files. Research has shown that students have more success when they initially focus on concepts rather than syntax, and our approach allows instructors to present material in a clear and illustrated manner that empowers rather than overwhelms the student.

ORGANIZATION AND COVERAGE

A Guide to Working with Visual Logic provides a hands-on, minimal syntax introduction to programming fundamentals. Chapter 1 covers input, assignment, and output statements. These three commands are sufficient for students to write a variety of simple but interesting programs. This chapter also introduces variables and expressions. Chapter 2 explains the role of conditional statements and the decision-making ability programs can have when conditions are used. This chapter also uses a case study to illustrate that there is more than one correct solution to a problem.

Chapters 3 and 4 present the concept of loops or iterative actions. Sequential (Chapter 1), conditional (Chapter 2), and iterative (Chapter 3) actions are sufficient to write any computer program. Students are also introduced to Console I/O which provides a full, persistent history of the input and output for a program's execution. Sentinel values, as well as nested loops, are introduced and numerous examples are presented in both chapters to help students develop a strong understanding of these critical control structures.

Chapter 5 introduces the power of arrays for holding and manipulating structured data. The chapter emphasizes the way that For loops and arrays are often used together, and there are again numerous examples to help students solidify their understanding of the power of arrays. The notion of File I/O is also introduced in this chapter, giving students yet another way to get data to and from their program.

Chapter 6 introduces both Graphics and Procedures. Our experience has been that these two topics are complementary and that presenting them together is beneficial to students. Using procedures to repeatedly call a series of related graphical commands gives the student a visual confirmation of the power and utility of procedures. Arguments and parameters are used to specify the location and size of the graphical objects being drawn. The chapter also includes an example of a recursive graphical procedure to visual demonstration how code can be used to call itself.

Finally, three appendices identify a list of Visual Logic reserved words, provide debugging strategies and techniques, and open the door to more creative problem solving using multimedia elements in a Visual Logic solution file.

FEATURES OF THE TEXT

Case Study Scenario and Solution—The Case Study Scenarios are used to promote problem-based learning. Scenarios present the student with a challenging programming problem whose solution requires skills the student has not yet developed. These skills are presented as the chapter unfolds, and then the Case Study Solution is presented that solves the scenario problem. The scenarios all involve a creative and fun-loving instructor, Mr. Taylor, and his interactions with students in his introductory programming class.

Ask the Author—Common student questions are asked and answered in the appropriate learning context. These questions help the student stay engaged with the material and are used to identify and dispel common areas of misconception.

Quick Checks—Quick check problems appear throughout the text to provide readers with an opportunity to apply their knowledge.

Tell Me More—These elements provide a business or applied perspective on the current topic.

Tips—These provide additional information or clarification to improve the student's learning experience.

Figures—Screen shots of programs during execution are frequently included. Students see GUI and console sample screens to show just how input and output will look.

Topic Summary—Following each major topic is a summary that recaps the programming concepts and techniques students should remember for that topic. This feature reinforces key ideas before moving on to new material.

Chapter Summary—Each chapter concludes with a complete summary of the terms and ideas introduced in the chapter. This feature provides a concise means for students to review and check their understanding of the main points in each chapter.

Key Terms—Each chapter lists key terms. Along with the chapter summary, the list of key terms provides a snapshot overview of a chapter's main ideas.

Review Questions—Review questions appear at the end of every chapter to allow students to test their comprehension of the major ideas and techniques presented.

Programming Exercises—Exercises are included so students have more opportunities for hands-on programming practice of concepts they have learned in that chapter.

VISUAL LOGIC™

This book is a guide to the software program called **Visual Logic**™. Visual Logic is a simple but powerful tool for teaching programming logic and design without traditional high-level programming language syntax. Visual Logic uses flowcharts to explain essential programming concepts, including variables, input, assignment, output, conditions, loops, procedures, graphics, arrays, and files. It also has the ability to interpret and execute flowcharts, providing students with immediate and accurate feedback about their solutions. By executing student solutions, Visual Logic combines the power of a high-level language with the ease and simplicity of flowcharts.

Visual Logic runs on any of the following Windows operating systems: 98, NT, 2000, ME, XP, or Vista. The minimum requirements for Windows also satisfy the minimum requirements for Visual Logic. Visual Logic may be purchased along with your text. Please contact your Course Technology sales representative for more information.

ACKNOWLEDGMENTS

First of all, we want to thank you, the students and instructors who use our book. We are honored that you chose us.

We would also like to thank the fine people at Course Technology. In particular, Managing Editor Tricia Coia and Acquisitions Editor Amy Jollymore both provided excellent vision and direction, always providing valuable insight when surveying the forest as well as when inspecting the individual trees. Others who stand out include Marie Lee, Jill Braiewa, Chris Scriver, and Danielle Shaw. We are delighted to be working with Course Technology on this (and other) projects.

We are also very grateful to the instructors who have used Visual Logic as a stand-alone product while this Guide was under development. We knew this book would eventually be available to complement the software, but things often take longer than anticipated. Thank you for your patience and we hope you will find this book to be worth the wait.

We also acknowledge the development team at VisualLogic.org and appreciate their support with this book. They have set up an e-mail address that you can use to comment on this book, including what you like and what we can do better in future editions. Please send e-mail to Guide@VisualLogic.org. We look forward to hearing from you.

Finally, we dedicate this book to our families for their unfailing love and support, and who join with us in thanking God for His many blessings.

— Thad Crews

— Chip Murphy

INPUT, PROCESS, OUTPUT

》CASE STUDY SCENARIO

Grocery Checkout

Mr. Marion Taylor's programming course is one of the most popular classes on campus: students appreciate Mr. Taylor's knowledge of the material and passion for teaching. In the minutes before the first class begins, Mr. Taylor and his students discuss movies, sports, and the parking problem on campus.

At the first class meeting, Mr. Taylor takes roll and hands out the syllabus, then asks, "How many of you have ever written a computer program before?" A few students raise their hands. "How many of you are ready to learn how to program?" Most of the class raises their hands. Looking around the room, Mr. Taylor smiles and says, "Well, the best way to learn programming is to program. Today we will cover input, processing, and output statements. After discussing these three statements, we will develop a working grocery checkout program. Our solution will input the purchase price of three items in the store. The program will determine the total price of all three items, add 6 percent sales tax, and display the resulting total." After a short pause for effect, he adds, "Oh yeah, and we will finish the program with enough time left in class for me to tell a bad joke."

Mr. Taylor's solution is presented later this chapter.

INTRODUCTION

A **computer program** is a solution to a problem, such as, "How can customers view and purchase products over the Internet?" or "How can sales representatives have immediate and accurate access to inventory data?"

Most useful computer programs typically do at least three things: input data, process data, and output resulting information (see Figure 1-1).

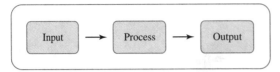

Figure 1-1 Input-Process-Output

For example, an online catalog information system might have input that includes the product ID for the items a customer wishes to purchase, along with the customer's mailing address and credit card number. The processing could include referencing a database to determine the cost of each item, calculating the sales tax, computing the shipping charge based on the customer's mailing address, and billing the customer's credit card the appropriate amount. The output might include a customer receipt and reports for the sales department and the warehouse (see Figure 1-2).

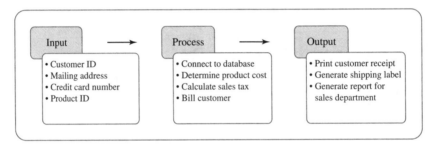

Figure 1-2 Input-Process-Output for an Internet shopping cart system

LOGIC AND SYNTAX

Building a software application is often compared to building a house. First you decide what kind of house you want (ranch, A-frame, tri-level, etc.) and what features you want (privacy, lots of sunlight, good for entertaining, etc.). Then you design a house blueprint that achieves all of the objectives. The blueprint design must be detailed, not only containing the complete floor plan, but also containing a description of all electrical and plumbing information. When the design is finalized, then the construction can begin. If you have a good design being worked on by skilled professionals (carpenters, plumbers, electricians, brick layers, etc.), the house should turn out great.

Would you consider building a house without a blueprint? Of course not! (What a terrible house that would be.) The same is true for programming. Software professionals would never build an important piece of software (such as an air traffic control system or an online banking system) without first having a blueprint for the software. An **algorithm** is the logical blueprint for software. Various tools for representing computing algorithms are available, the two most common being flowcharts and pseudocode. In this book we will use **Visual Logic**™, which combines the graphics of flowcharts (graphical representations of algorithms) and the utility of pseudocode (a minimal syntax description of an algorithm) into a single simulation tool. Using Visual Logic, you will create computer algorithms that can be saved, edited, executed, and debugged.

Once an algorithm has been developed, it must be communicated in an appropriate language. To communicate actions to a computer, developers use a programming language like Visual Basic, C#, C++, Java, Pascal, or COBOL (among others). Syntax refers to the specific rules of a programming language. There are literally hundreds of programming languages to choose from, each with its own unique syntax. Therefore, writing a computer program involves first creating a logical solution to solve a problem and then implementing that solution in an appropriate syntax.

)) TELL ME MORE

An algorithm is not limited to computer programs. Driving directions, a cooking recipe, and the rules to play Monopoly are all everyday examples of algorithms.

Consider the instructions to bake a cake. The algorithm (or steps) include adding eggs, mixing ingredients, and cooking at a specific temperature. These basic steps can be stated in various languages. For example, the step of adding two eggs can be stated in English ("Add two eggs"), Spanish ("Agregue dos huevos"), or French ("Ajouter deux oeufs"). The result is the same regardless of the language.

Likewise, the logic of an Internet shopping cart remains essentially the same regardless of its implementation language (Visual Basic, C#, C++, Java, Pascal, COBOL, etc.).

Of course the process (e.g., algorithm) for selling products over the Internet is more complicated than baking a cake, but it is still eventually broken down to a series of steps to accomplish the objective.

ASK THE AUTHOR

Q: What is the difference between data and information?

A: From an information system perspective, data refers to numbers, characters, or images without context. Data by itself has no meaning. When data is processed in a context (either by a human or a computer system) it becomes information. As information is collected, it can also be processed for patterns and insights, thus creating knowledge. Finally, wisdom is appropriate behavior guided by knowledge. Consider the following example as it applies to a screen-printing company's online purchasing system.

» "5000" is data.

» "A 5000 percent increase in T-shirt orders by Gizmo Company" is information.

» "A 5000 percent increase in T-shirt orders by any company is an unusually large increase" is knowledge.

» "We had better confirm the numbers on this order before we manufacture and ship the T-shirts, just to make sure it was not a human or system mistake" is wisdom.

YOUR FIRST PROGRAM: HELLO WORLD

It is a time-honored tradition that your first program in any language be the output message "Hello World." We will follow suit and write a Hello World program using Visual Logic.

Begin by running the Visual Logic program contained on the CD-ROM included with this text. When the program begins, you will see two flowcharting elements, Begin and End, connected by a flow-arrow. Click the left mouse button on the flow-arrow; the Flowchart Elements menu should pop up (Figure 1-3).

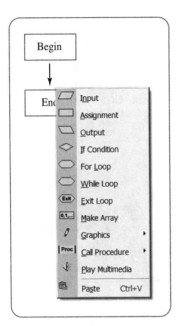

Figure 1-3 Flowchart Elements menu

Select Output from the pop-up menu to add an output element to your flowchart. Then double-click on the newly added output element, opening the output dialog box. Type **"Hello World"** (make sure that you include the double quotes) in the text box, and then click the OK button. Figure 1-4 shows how your flowchart should look after closing the dialog box.

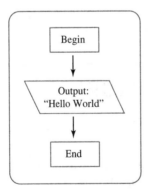

Figure 1-4 Hello World solution

Press F5 to run the program. The program executes, generating an output dialog box that appears with the text "Hello World" (Figure 1-5). Congratulations! You have just written your first computer program!

Figure 1-5 Hello World simulation output

YOUR SECOND PROGRAM: HELLO NAME

Remember that an information system must input data, process data, and output resulting information. The first of those three tasks, inputting data into the system, is accomplished by means of an input statement. An **input statement** accepts data from the user and stores that data into a variable. A **variable** is a storage location that can be accessed and changed by developer code. A variable has a name (which does not change) and an associated data value (which may change during execution).

To understand the input statement, consider the following modification to the Hello World program you just wrote. Click on the flow-arrow above the output statement and add an input element. Double-click on the input element, opening the input element dialog box. Type **Name** (without quotes) in the variable text box and press OK. Then double-click on the output element and edit the text in the dialog box to read **"Hello " & Name** (being sure to include quotes around "Hello " followed by the ampersand [&] symbol followed by the unquoted Name variable). Your solution should now look like Figure 1-6.

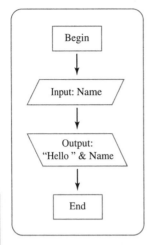

Figure 1-6 Hello Name solution

Run the program. You will be prompted to type a value for Name. Enter your name inside double quotes (e.g., "Dave"). The program will then display a message box with the appropriate greeting (e.g., "Hello Dave"; see Figure 1-7).

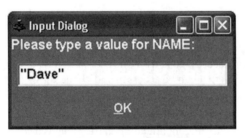

Figure 1-7 One possible output of the Hello Name program

SIMPLE PROGRAMMING FORMATS

The Hello Name program uses an input statement to prompt the user for a value that is stored and then reused in an output statement. The value entered at the input prompt can be either numeric (e.g., 42 or 3.14159) or a string (e.g., "Abraham Lincoln" or "Merry Christmas"). Be aware that string input data must be contained within quotes.

There are some constraints with numeric data as well. Most programming languages do not allow numeric input to include symbols such as the percent symbol (%) or dollar sign ($) or even commas (,). Numeric input should consist of only digits and possibly one decimal point. You will quickly get used to using proper numeric notations for programming. Table 1-1 summarizes some common numeric notations and the correct programming format.

Value	Written format	Programming format	Comment
String	Hello World	`"Hello World"`	Use quotes to delimit strings
Percent	15%	`0.15`	Use decimal format
Dollars	$300	`300`	Dollar signs not allowed
Large numbers	12,345,678	`12345678`	Commas not allowed

Table 1-1 Common notations with correct programming formats

VARIABLE SUMMARY

» Variables are storage locations used for holding data and information.

» Each variable has two components: its name (which does not change) and its value (which may change during execution).

INPUT STATEMENT SUMMARY

» Input statements are used to get data into variables.

» In Visual Logic, the input flowchart element is a parallelogram with the keyword Input followed by the variable name.

» When the input statement is executed, the user is prompted to enter a value using the keyboard. The value typed is then stored in the variable for later use.

» String input must be placed inside quotes.

» Numeric input must contain only digits and possibly one decimal point. Percent symbols (%), dollar signs ($), and commas (,), among other symbols, are not allowed.

WEEKLY PAYCHECK PROGRAM

You have now written your first two computer programs, Hello World and Hello Name. Your third program will be a bit more complicated. You will now write a weekly paycheck program that accepts the hours worked and the hourly rate for an employee, and the program will calculate and display the appropriate pay amount due to the employee for the current week. This weekly paycheck program will use all three basics of an information system—input, processing, and output—and will be developed in steps.

STEP 1: INPUT

The weekly paycheck program has two input variables, *Hours* and *Rate*. Start Visual Logic. (If it is already running, under the menu click File, then New.) Click on the flow-arrow and select the input element. Repeat to add a second input element. Then double-click on each element to add the variable names Hours and Rate (Figure 1-8). These two elements are the input for the weekly paycheck program.

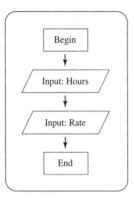

Figure 1-8 Partial weekly paycheck
solution (input only)

ASK THE AUTHOR

Q: You used **Hours** and **Rate** as variable names. Could you have chosen different names?

A: Yes. You have a great deal of freedom when it comes to naming variables. However, below are some suggestions and rules to remember:

1. A variable name should be descriptive of the data it holds.

2. A variable name must begin with a letter.

3. Only letters, digits, or the underscore character (_) may be used in variable names. Uppercase and lowercase do not matter. This means that **HOURS, hours**, and **Hours** are all interchangeable. In this book we will use the convention of starting each word in a variable name with an uppercase letter (e.g., **Cost, MailingAddress, ZipCode**).

4. The variable name must not be a word that is reserved by the programming language for other special uses. A list of reserved words can be found in Appendix A.

STEP 2: PROCESSING

The assignment statement can be used to perform a calculation and store the result. Addition (+), subtraction (−), multiplication (*), and division (/) are common arithmetic operations found in almost every high-level programming language. Note that the multiplication operator is typically an asterisk (*) rather than the traditional times operator (x), because X could be mistaken as a variable name.

To illustrate the use of the assignment statement, we return to the weekly paycheck program. You have already used two input statements to accept the data Hours and Rate. You will now add an assignment statement to process that data. The required calculation is straightforward. Hours times rate produces the pay amount due.

Returning to Visual Logic, click on a flow-arrow below the two input statements, and then select an assignment element from the menu. Double-click the assignment element to open the assignment edit dialog. The text box on the left is labeled *Variable*, and the text box on the right is labeled *Expression*. An **expression** is a value-returning code element, such as a variable or mathematical formula. Most programming languages follow this tradition of specifying the expression on the right-hand side (RHS) of the assignment statement, and specifying the variable to store the result on the left-hand side (LHS) of the assignment statement. When executed, the right-hand side expression is evaluated first. The result of the expression is then stored into the left-hand side variable.

Enter **Hours * Rate** in the right-hand expression text box and **Pay** in the left-hand text box. When finished, your solution should look like Figure 1-9. Your program now accepts two input values and performs an appropriate calculation based on those input values.

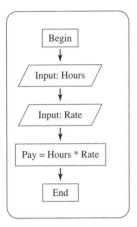

Figure 1-9 Partial weekly paycheck solution (input and assignment)

ASSIGNMENT STATEMENT SUMMARY

» Assignment statements are used to perform calculations and store the result.

» In Visual Logic, the assignment flowchart element is a rectangle with a variable on the left-hand side (LHS) and an expression on the right-hand side (RHS).

» When executed, the expression is evaluated, and the result is stored in the variable.

STEP 3: OUTPUT

Output can occur in many forms. Two common types of output are screen output and printed (i.e., hardcopy) output, both of which are visual. Sound output is common through speakers. Output involving the other senses (touch, smell, and taste) are possible as well. Information saved to a storage device such as a floppy disk, hard disk, or CD is also considered to be a form of output.

We conclude the paycheck program by adding an output dialog that displays an appropriate message to the user. Add an output element to your flowchart, and then double-click the element to enter the output expression. In the text box, type:

"Pay amount due is " & FormatCurrency(Pay)

Your completed flowchart should look like Figure 1-10.

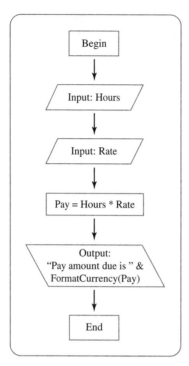

Figure 1-10 Weekly paycheck solution

Press F5 to run the program. The program prompts the user to enter a value for hours, then prompts the user again for a value for rate. The calculation is made and the information is displayed to the user in an output dialog box. For example, Figure 1-11 shows the output generated by input values of 30 hours and 8 dollars per hour rate.

Figure 1-11 Weekly paycheck solution output

Congratulations! You have just written your third computer program! Save this program, as we will revise it in Chapter 2. (To save the file, select the menu option File | Save to create a .vls file, which is the Visual Logic solution file format.)

ASK THE AUTHOR

Q: You mentioned touch, smell, and taste output. Are you serious? If so, who is doing these kinds of things?

A: Yes, full sensory output is a real area of exploration. Various tactile (e.g., touch) output is already available, such as force-feedback game controllers or dynamic Braille.

As for the "Who?" part of your question, there are traditionally two groups. First are the scientists and inventors who are trying to do new and different things just to see if it can be done. Then there are the entrepreneurs who use new technologies to create business opportunities. For example, a perfume company may want to make samples of their products available online. Likewise, a clothing company may want to give Internet visitors the opportunity to feel the texture of the products as they shop. Most of these technologies are still experimental. Nonetheless, it is a real possibility that you will use all five senses when you browse the Internet in 2020.

HOW TO WRITE ARITHMETIC EXPRESSIONS

The calculation in the weekly paycheck program is rather straightforward (hours times rate). As a developer, you will often have to perform calculations that are significantly more complex. Visual Logic supports seven arithmetic operators, evaluated in the order of operator precedence shown in Table 1-2. Operators of the same precedence are evaluated left to right. Parentheses can be used to override the default precedence order.

There are three operators related to division. Regular division (/) produces a decimal value if necessary. Integer division (\) and integer remainder (Mod) require integer arguments and produce an integer answer. Integer division is the integer result, throwing away any remainder. Integer remainder is the amount left over after taking out as many whole occurrences of the numerator from the divisor as possible.

Operation	Operator	Expression1	Result1	Expression2	Result2
Exponentiation	^	5 ^ 2 + 1	26	5 ^ (2 + 1)	125
Multiplication and division	* /	1 + 3 * 7	22	17 / 3	5.667
Integer division	\	12 \ 4	3	17 \ 3	5
Integer remainder	Mod	12 Mod 4	0	17 Mod 3	2
Addition and subtraction	+ -	4 - 5 + 2	1	4 - (5 + 2)	-3

Table 1-2 Numeric operator precedence, highest to lowest

》》TELL ME MORE

Integer division and integer remainder are new operators to most students. Once you understand them, you will find they can be used in a variety of situations. For example, you can determine if a number is even or odd using the integer remainder operator. If **N Mod 2** is 0, then N is even. If not, then N is odd.

For another example, consider the everyday task of giving correct change. If you were owed 82 cents in change, you typically would not expect 82 pennies. Instead, you would expect 3 quarters, 1 nickel, and 2 pennies. A developer can use an expression like **Amount \ 25** to determine how many quarters are appropriate, and **Amount MOD 25** would calculate the change remaining after the quarters have been given. Additional integer division and integer remainder expressions could calculate the number of dimes, nickels, and pennies.

QUICK CHECK 1-A

Evaluate each of the following mathematical expressions. Assume $A = 3$, $B = 5$.

1. A + B * 5
2. (2 * 3) ^ 2
3. 11 \ A
4. 2 * 3 ^2
5. 11 / A
6. 11 Mod A

QUICK CHECK 1-B

Write Visual Logic expressions for each of the following.

1. The average of Exam 1, Exam 2, and Exam 3

2. $1 + \frac{1}{2} + \frac{1}{4}$

3. $\dfrac{4A^2B}{C}$

STRATEGIES FOR DOING CONVERSIONS

One area where it is easy to make a mistake is when performing a calculation to convert from one unit of measurement to another. Consider the seemingly simple task of converting inches to feet. Below are the incorrect and correct versions of this calculation.

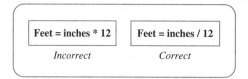

Feet = inches * 12	Feet = inches / 12
Incorrect	*Correct*

To understand why the first assignment is incorrect and the second is correct, consider the situation where inches has the value of 24. Since 24 inches is 2 feet, the correct value for feet should be 2. The first example above would calculate 24 * 12 and assign the result (288) to feet, which is almost the size of a football field. The second example would calculate 24/12 and assign the result (2) to feet, which is of course the correct answer.

INTRINSIC FUNCTIONS

The weekly paycheck solution uses the intrinsic function FormatCurrency to display a numeric value in a currency format, including a leading dollar sign, two decimal places, and delimiting commas as necessary. Intrinsic functions are predefined commands that provide developers with common, helpful functionality. Intrinsic functions are divided into several categories, including math functions, business functions, string functions, time and date functions, conversion functions, file access functions, and so on. Another intrinsic function is FormatPercent, which takes a decimal percent value and converts it to its equivalent value with a percent symbol and two decimal places. Abs accepts a numeric value and produces the absolute value equivalent. Int accepts a decimal value and produces the integer whole value. Round accepts a decimal value and produces the nearest integer value. Finally, Random accepts an integer value N and produces a random integer between 0 and (N−1). Table 1-3 shows examples of these intrinsic functions.

Example	Result
FormatCurrency(12345)	$12,345.00
FormatCurrency(.02)	$0.02
FormatPercent(0.0625)	6.25%
FormatPercent(0.75)	75.00%
Abs(-3.3)	3.3
Abs(5.67)	5.67
Int(3.8)	3
Int(7.1)	7
Round(3.8)	4
Round(7.1)	7
Random(5)	A random integer between 0 and 4
Random(100) + 1	A random integer between 1 and 100

Table 1-3 Intrinsic functions for Visual Logic

OUTPUT STATEMENT SUMMARY
» Output statements are used to display information.
» In Visual Logic, the output flowchart element is a parallelogram with the keyword Output followed by an output expression.

» When executed, string literals are displayed exactly as typed inside the containing quotes.

» When executed, expressions are evaluated and the result is displayed.

» The ampersand (&) operator may be used to concatenate a series of string literals, variables, and expressions into one large expression.

» Carriage returns in the output expression appear as carriage returns in the displayed output.

DEBUGGING WITH VISUAL LOGIC

Even the best developers will eventually make mistakes. A programming mistake is often called a **bug** (see Tell Me More box, below), although the term error is probably more appropriate. Visual Logic provides debugging support to help you track down and fix your errors. Figure 1-12 shows the execution and debugging portion of the Visual Logic standard toolbar. Note that these functions are also available under the Debug menu item. *Run* is the command that executes the simulator. *Pause* stops the simulation on the current command. *Terminate* ends the execution of the current program.

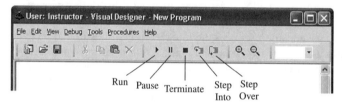

Figure 1-12 Execution and debugging in the Visual Logic toolbar

The last two options, *Step Into* and *Step Over*, allow a paused program to execute one step at a time. When the program is paused, the Variable Watch window appears displaying the current values for all program variables. Step Into takes you to the next command and will go into a structure like a condition or a loop (which we discuss in the following chapters). Step Over takes you to the next command at the same level as the current command. Using the step commands to study the program variable values as each statement executes can be helpful in determining why your program is generating an error. For more information about debugging, see Appendix B.

»TELL ME MORE

There is an interesting history behind the term **bug**. The term may have arisen as early as the fourteenth century to mean "an object of dread" derived from the Welsh word *bwg* for hobgoblin. Thomas Edison is quoted as using the term bugs for flaws in a system in 1878.

The term became particularly popular in 1947 when a moth was found in a relay of the Harvard Mark II machine. Grace Murray Hopper (who later helped design COBOL and is affectionately knows as the "Mother of Modern Computing") was involved in the project. She once related the events as follows, "Things were going badly; there was something wrong in one of the circuits of the long glass-enclosed computer.

Finally, someone located the trouble spot and, using ordinary tweezers, removed the problem, a two-inch moth. From then on, when anything went wrong with a computer, we said it had bugs in it."

The moth was taped in the computer log, with the following entry: *"First actual case of bug being found."* The logbook, now in the collection of Naval Surface Weapons Center, still contains the remains of the moth.

(Additional Source: The AFU and Urban Legends Archive. "Have Some Grace and Don't Let it Bug You," http://www.tafkac.org/faq2k/compute_86.html)

>> CASE STUDY SOLUTION

Grocery Checkout

"Now it's time to put our new knowledge to the test," Mr. Taylor says 10 minutes before the class ends. "We have discussed how Visual Logic can be used to do input, processing, and output. Our grocery checkout problem requires three input values (the prices of the three items), three calculations (the subtotal of the three items, the appropriate sales tax, and the resulting total), and a single output (the resulting total). Let me show you how this can be done in Visual Logic." Below are the steps Mr. Taylor follows when demonstrating the solution for the class.

1. From the Visual Logic menu, select File | New to start a new program. Add three input elements to your flowchart. Enter the variable names **Item1**, **Item2**, and **Item3** respectively.

2. Add an assignment element to your flowchart. Enter **SubTotal** as the result variable, and enter **Item1 + Item2 + Item3** as the expression.

3. Add a second assignment element to your flowchart. Set the variable **SalesTax** to be the result of the expression **SubTotal * 0.06**.

4. Add a third assignment element that sets **Total** to be the sum of **SubTotal + SalesTax**.

5. Display the Total with an appropriate output statement. Your solution should look something like Figure 1-13.

6. Run your program to see if it works. If the input values are 10, 20, and 30, the output should be "Your purchase total is $63.60."

The class works on their programs getting help from Mr. Taylor as needed. Finally, just as class is about to end, a student from the back of the class shouts, "What about the bad joke?"

Mr. Taylor considers for a moment, then says "What did the termite say when he went into the bar?" (pause) "Where is the bar tender?"

A couple of students laugh and explain the joke to their neighbors. Others are confused, not sure if it was supposed to be funny or not. "Don't quit your day job," one student says.

"Not a chance," Mr. Taylor says, smiling.

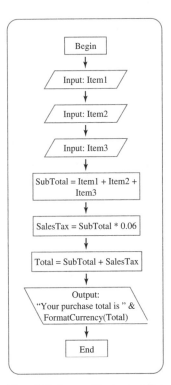

Figure 1-13 Grocery Checkout solution

CHAPTER SUMMARY

» Variables are storage locations used for holding data and information.

» Each variable has two components: its name (which does not change) and its value (which may change during execution).

» Input statements are used to get data into variables. When executed, the user is prompted to enter a value using the keyboard. The value typed is then stored in the variable for later use.

» Expressions are value-returning code elements, such as a variable or mathematical formula.

» Assignment statements are used to perform calculations and store the result. When an assignment statement is executed, the expression is evaluated and the result is stored in the variable.

» Output statements are used to display information. When an output statement is executed, string literals are displayed exactly as typed inside the containing quotes, and expressions are evaluated and the result is displayed. The ampersand (&) operator may be used to concatenate a series of string literals and expressions into one large expression.

» Input, assignment, and output statements are sufficient to write small but interesting computer programs.

KEY TERMS

algorithm	expression	output statement
assignment statement	input statement	syntax
bug	intrinsic function	variable
computer program	knowledge	wisdom
data	operator precedence	

REVIEW QUESTIONS

1. Consider the similarities and differences between developing an algorithm and developing syntax. What skills are required for each activity? What is the added value for each activity?

2. Identify possible input, processing, and output for a video store's rental checkout system.

3. Imagine you are an entrepreneur with access to some of the innovative output technologies regarding smell, touch, and taste. Identify some business uses of these technologies that you think might become profitable.

PROGRAMMING EXERCISES

1-1. A Rose by Any Other Name. Paulette has just planted a large rose garden that she wants to fertilize. She knows the area of her rose garden in square feet, but the fertilizer is measured by the square yard. Write a program that converts square feet to square yards. (*Hint*: Make sure you are using the correct conversion ratio. Most everyone knows 3 feet makes 1 yard. Are square feet and square yards any different?)

Input Variable	Process/Output Variable
SquareFeet	SquareYards

1-2. Twenty Thousand Leagues Under the Sea. Jules Verne's book <u>Twenty Thousand Leagues Under the Sea</u> is the story of Captain Nemo and his fantastic submarine *Nautilus*. The story is told from the perspective of Professor Aronnax, who entered the Nautilus as a prisoner but later is treated as a guest. At one point the professor writes, "I have crossed 20,000 leagues in that submarine tour of the world, which has revealed so many wonders." Write a program that will input a distance in leagues and then calculate and display that same distance in nautical miles. (*Hint*: Perform an Internet search to find the conversion ratio between leagues and nautical miles.)

Input Variable	Process/Output Variable
Leagues	NauticalMiles

1-3. Run the Numbers. Write a program with two input values. The program should display the sum, difference, quotient, product, and average of the two numbers.

Input Variables	Process/Output Variables
Num1, Num2	Sum, Difference, Quotient, Product, Average

1-4. Gross and Net Pay. Write a program with two input values, Hours and Rate. The program should first calculate Gross pay, which is your pay before deductions. The program should then calculate the following three deduction amounts: Federal Tax (20% of Gross), State Tax (5% of Gross), Social Security Tax (6.2% of Gross). Then your program should calculate Net pay, which is your Gross pay minus the three deductions. The output should be all five of the calculated values.

Input Variables	Process/Output Variables
Hours, Rate	GrossPay, FederalTax, StateTax, SocialSecurity, NetPay

1-5. "As I was going to St. Ives . . . " Consider the following nursery rhyme:

As I was going to St. Ives, I met a man with seven wives. Every wife had seven sacks, every sack had seven cats, and every cat had seven kittens. Kittens, cats, sacks, and wives, how many were going to St. Ives?

The question at the end of the rhyme is a trick question because only the narrator is going to St. Ives. Write a program to determine the total number of things (including people, animals, and sacks) that were met by the narrator.

Input Variable	Process/Output Variables
(none required; it is all provided in the rhyme)	Man, Wives, Sacks, Cats, Kittens

1-6. Correct Change. Write a program to assist a cashier with determining correct change. The program should have one input, the number of cents to return to the customer. The output should be the appropriate change in quarters, dimes, nickels and cents.

(*Hint*: Consider how integer division (\) and integer remainder (Mod) can be used as part of your solution.)

Input Variable	Process/Output Variables
Change	Quarters, Dimes, Nickels, Pennies

1-7. Jake's Problem. Jake has a car with an 8-gallon fuel tank. Jake fills his tank with gas and then drives 60 miles to a friend's house. When he gets to his friend's house, he has 6 gallons left in his fuel tank. Write a program that uses three input elements to enter values for tank size, miles traveled, and gallons left. The program should calculate and display how many miles Jake can drive on a full tank of gas. (*Note*: Be sure to use input elements to accept the values 8, 60, and 6 rather than hard-coding them into your solution.)

Input Variables	Process/Output Variables
TankSize, MilesTraveled, GallonsLeft	*(left to the reader)*

MAKING DECISIONS

MAKING DECISIONS

In the previous chapter we developed a program for calculating a weekly paycheck. The amount due was calculated using a simple assignment statement:

$$\textbf{Pay} = \textbf{Hours} * \textbf{Rate}$$

This calculation works fine under normal circumstances. However, it is a common practice for many businesses to give overtime pay to employees who work more than 40 hours in a week. The formula for calculating pay with overtime is 40 hours at regular pay plus hours over 40 at one-and-a-half times regular pay. This can be easily expressed in an assignment statement, as follows:

$$\textbf{Pay} = \textbf{40 * Rate} + \textbf{(Hours} - \textbf{40) * Rate * 1.5}$$

The "Normal" formula works for regular pay, and the "Overtime" formula works for overtime pay. Unfortunately, neither formula works in all situations. What is needed, therefore, is a way for the program to choose which formula is appropriate. In other words, the program needs to make a decision.

ASK THE AUTHOR

Q: What kind of decisions can a computer make?

A: A computer's decision-making process is limited because each of the computer's possible actions must be specified in advance. Humans have the ability to be creative, but a computer can only select between predefined actions based on the result of some evaluation. Those with an interest in the history of computing may find it interesting that Edward Dijkstra used the term "selection" when referring to the computer's ability to make decisions (see the following Tell Me More entry).

» TELL ME MORE

Edward Dijkstra was one of the most influential persons in the history of computer programming. His article "Structured programming" (first published in *Software Engineering Techniques*, 1970) demonstrated that any logical programming solution might be expressed using only three control flow constructs: sequential, selection, and repetition. Sequential commands (e.g., input, assignment, and output) were presented in Chapter 1 of this textbook. This chapter is about Selection, and Chapter 3 is about Repetition. By mastering these three constructs, programmers can create code in which the logical design is evident on inspection, thus making solutions easier to develop, test, and maintain.

THE IF STATEMENT

The most common selection (or "decision") structure is the **IF statement**. The IF statement begins with a condition, followed by a block of statements that execute only when the condition evaluates to true, and an optional block of statements that execute only when the condition evaluates to false. The two blocks are called the true block and the false block (for obvious reasons). The IF statement ends where the two blocks reconnect.

A **condition** is a boolean expression that evaluates to either true or false. Conditions typically involve one of the six **relational operators** shown in Table 2-1.

Operator	Description	Expression	Result (*assume x* = 2, *y* = 3)
=	Equal	x = 2	True
		x = y	False
<>	Not Equal	y <> 5	True
		y <> 3	False
>	Greater Than	x > 1	True
		x > y	False
<	Less Than	x < y	True
		x < 2	False
>=	Greater Than Or Equal	x >= 2	True
		x >= y	False
<=	Less Than Or Equal	x <= 2	True
		x <= 1	False

Table 2-1 Relational operators

QUICK CHECK 2-A

Evaluate each of the following conditions. Assume A = 2, B = 6.

1. A < B
2. A = B
3. 17 Mod B <> 5
4. (A - B) = (B - A)
5. B + A * B = 18

SIMPLE IF STATEMENTS

To understand how an IF statement is used in Visual Logic, consider the simple problem of reading two values and determining if they are equal or not. Our solution will use two input statements followed by an IF statement to compare the two values. Add an output statement inside the true branch to display the message: **The values are equal**. Likewise, add an output statement inside the false branch to display the message: **The values are not equal** (see Figure 2-1). Run this solution multiple times with different input values to verify its behavior.

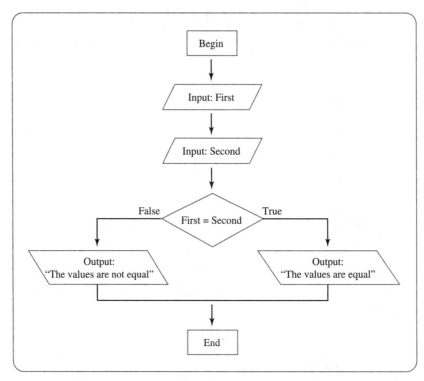

Figure 2-1 A simple IF statement

SOLVING THE OVERTIME PROBLEM

An IF statement can be used to solve the overtime problem. Specifically, the solution will make a decision about which formula is appropriate based on the number of hours worked by the employee.

From the Visual Logic menu, select File | Open. Open the file containing the paycheck program you saved from the previous chapter (see Figure 1-8). Click on the flow-arrow above the assignment statement, and add a condition element to your flowchart. Then double-click the element to enter the condition. In the text box, type the following condition:

Hours $<$ 40

Press OK to close the condition edit dialog box. Drag the existing assignment statement to the true branch and drop it there. Click the false branch and add a new assignment statement with the overtime formula. Your flowchart should now look like Figure 2-2. Run the program multiple times to ensure that the condition is working properly.

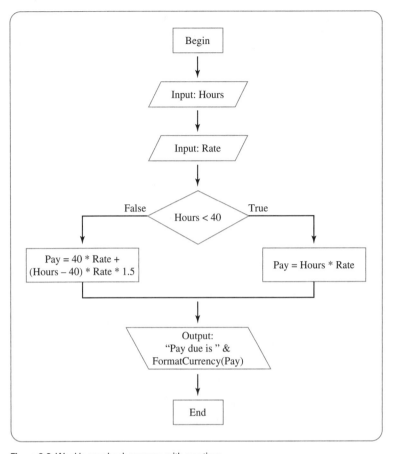

Figure 2-2 Weekly paycheck program with overtime

IF STATEMENT SUMMARY

» IF statements are used to choose between actions.

» In Visual Logic, the IF flowchart element is a diamond containing a condition and two exit arrows labeled True and False.

» A condition is a boolean expression, typically involving one of six relational operators.

» When executed, the condition is evaluated. If the condition is true, control flows along the true arrow. If the condition is false, control flows along the false arrow.

» An IF statement ends where the true and false branches reconnect.

NESTED IF STATEMENTS

The true and false branches of an IF statement may contain any number of statements of any type, including other IF statements. The term nested IF refers to an IF statement contained within the true or false branch of another IF statement.

To understand nested IF statements, consider the simple problem of reading two values and determining if they are equal, if the first is greater than the second, or if the first is smaller than the second. The three possible results are properly handled by the nested IF solution in Figure 2-3.

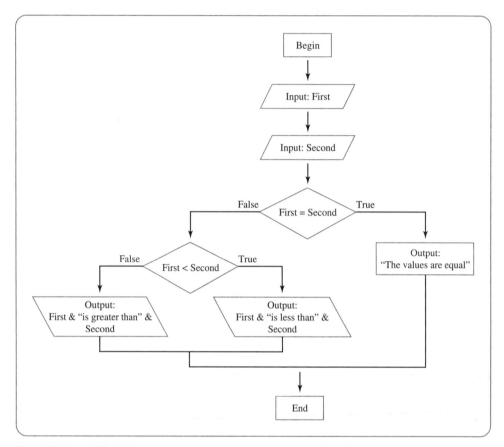

Figure 2-3 A nested IF solution

LONG-DISTANCE BILLING PROBLEM

Consider the problem of determining the billing rate for a long distance phone call. According to one billing plan, if a call is made between 6:00 a.m. and 6:00 p.m., then the billing rate should be 10 cents per minute. Nights and mornings are free. One possible solution to the billing requirement is shown in Figure 2-4. The problem assumes a military time format is being used (e.g., "1800" refers to 6:00 p.m.).

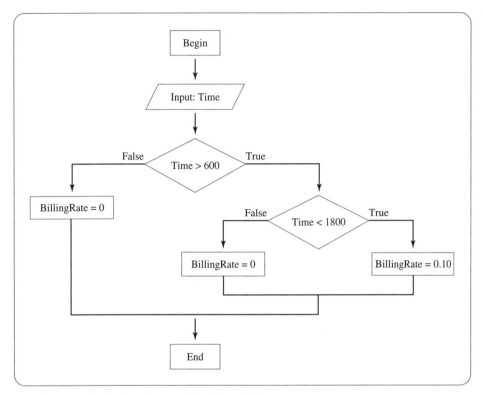

Figure 2-4 Nested IF solution to determine long-distance billing rate

COMPOUND CONDITIONS

When it comes to making decisions, developers are often faced with complex conditions that require multiple comparisons. A compound condition consists of two conditions within parentheses joined by a logical operator. The four most common logical operators are NOT, AND, OR, and XOR. Table 2-2 illustrates these four logical operators.

Operator	Description	Example	Result (*assume A = 5, B = 8*)
NOT	Returns the opposite of the condition	NOT (A < 3) NOT (B = 8)	True False
AND	Returns true if and only if both conditions are true	(A = 1) AND (B = 9) (A = 5) AND (B = 9) (A = 1) AND (B = 8) (A = 5) AND (B = 8)	False False False True
OR	Returns true if at least one condition is true	(A = 1) OR (B = 9) (A = 5) OR (B = 9) (A = 1) OR (B = 8) (A = 5) OR (B = 8)	False True True True
XOR	Returns true if the conditions have opposite values	(A = 1) XOR (B = 9) (A = 5) XOR (B = 9) (A = 1) XOR (B = 8) (A = 5) XOR (B = 8)	False True True False

Table 2-2 Logical operators with results

>> **TIP** Be sure to use parentheses around each condition when writing compound conditions. The parentheses make the conditions evaluate before the relational operator. If you do not use parentheses, then the result may not be what you expect. For example, the condition

(5 > 4) AND (4 > 3)

evaluates to True if you use parentheses; but it may evaluate incorrectly to False if you omit the parentheses.

To understand how compound conditions may be used, consider an automobile insurance company that charges a premium for male drivers under the age of 25. The condition that tests for this could be the following compound condition:

(Gender = "Male") AND (Age < 25)

Another example would be a test to see if a student is a senior (90 or more hours) with a grade point average at or above 3.25. The compound condition that tests for this would be:

(HoursEarned > 90) AND (GPA > 3.25)

There are times when a single compound condition can be used in place of a nested IF. For example, consider again the long-distance billing algorithm previously shown in Figure 2-4. This can be rewritten using a single compound condition, as shown in Figure 2-5. Both solutions are right because they both produce the correct result. It is a subjective opinion as to which, if either, is the better (e.g., more clear) solution.

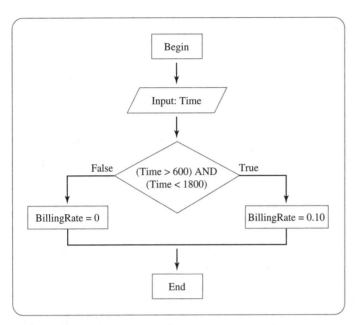

Figure 2-5 Compound condition solution to determine long-distance billing rate

Q: Are you saying there is no difference between the nested IF solution (Figure 2-4) and the compound condition solution (Figure 2-5) to the long-distance billing problem?

A: There are advantages and disadvantages with both. If the night and morning billing rate were to change, you would have to change two assignments in Figure 2-4 but only one in Figure 2-5, meaning the compound condition reduces the likelihood of a simple oversight error. On the other hand, using compound conditions requires caution because it is easy to use OR when AND is required and vice versa. What would happen in Figure 2-5 if the logical operator OR had been used instead of AND? (*Hint*: Customers would be unhappy.)

Generally speaking, it is a good idea to consider multiple solutions and choose the one that is clearest to you. The Case Study Solution will further illustrate this point.

QUICK CHECK 2-B

Evaluate each of the following compound conditions. Assume X = 3, Y = 7.

1. (X = 1) AND (Y = 7)

2. (X = 1) OR (Y = 7)

3. (X < Y) AND (Y > 10)

4. (X ^ 3 = 27) AND (Y Mod 2 = 1)

5. (X ^ 3 = 27) XOR (Y Mod 2 = 1)

▶ CASE STUDY SOLUTION

Smallest Number

Dr. Taylor continues, "Now that we have looked at IF statements, nested IF statements, and compound conditions, we can use these structures to write interesting programs. Consider the problem of inputting three unduplicated values and displaying the smallest value. We will examine four different solutions to this problem, all of which are correct. However, they are not necessarily equal."

John Paul speaks up, asking "If they are all correct, doesn't that make them equal?"

"Not necessarily. If, for example, one of the solutions is much easier to understand than the others, then that solution would be better. Given the choice, you should use the algorithm you understand best. In addition, some solutions lend themselves to modification better than others. Sometimes it is beneficial to consider alternative solutions rather than always using the first idea that comes to your mind."

Solution 1: Nested Conditions

Dr. Taylor hands out the first solution (Figure 2-6). "This first solution uses nested conditions. The first condition determines which is the smaller of A and B. The smaller of A and B is then compared with C via a nested condition. The smaller value of the second comparison is then displayed."

Solution 2: Compound Conditions

"This second solution (Figure 2-7) uses a series of compound conditions. The first compound condition checks to see if A holds the smallest value and, if so, prints A. Similar compound conditions are used for testing B and C. These conditions are sequential, not nested."

Solution 3: Nested and Compound Condition

"The third solution (Figure 2-8) to the smallest number problem begins with a compound condition. In this case, however, the program contains a nested condition in the false branch. Since A is not the smallest, the nested condition need only compare B and C to determine the smallest value."

Solution 4: Placeholder Variable

"Our fourth and final solution (Figure 2-9) takes a different approach than the first three. This solution makes use of an extra variable, **Smallest**, to serve as a placeholder for the smallest value. The placeholder is initially given the value of the first input number. Then each remaining input number is individually compared with the placeholder value. If a smaller number is found, the placeholder becomes the same as the newer, smaller value. After all values have been compared, the placeholder will hold the smallest of the input values."

Wrap-up

"All four of these solutions for finding the smallest number are correct. Which one is most clear?" The ensuing discussion is lively with a variety of opinions presented. The solutions are evaluated for how well they would handle slight variations on the problem. For example, what if duplicate values were allowed? What if the middle value were required instead of the smallest value? What if the size of the input was more than three values? The general consensus is that each solution has its advantages and that different solutions lend themselves better to different variations of the original problem. Looking at his watch, Dr. Taylor wraps up the conversation. "Comparing the strengths and weaknesses of multiple solutions is a key skill for writing great software. I think you are all doing an excellent job."

ASK THE AUTHOR

Q: In both Figures 2-7 and 2-8 you have a condition that reads:

$$(A < B) \text{ AND } (A < C)$$

Could this have also been written as: $(A < B < C)$?

A: No. The condition $(A < B < C)$ will not evaluate correctly. For your program to work properly, you need two explicit tests $(A < B)$ and $(A < C)$, and you need to join those two tests using the compound AND operator, as shown in Figure 2-6 and Figure 2-7. Also remember to include parentheses around the two conditions to ensure the AND evaluates properly.

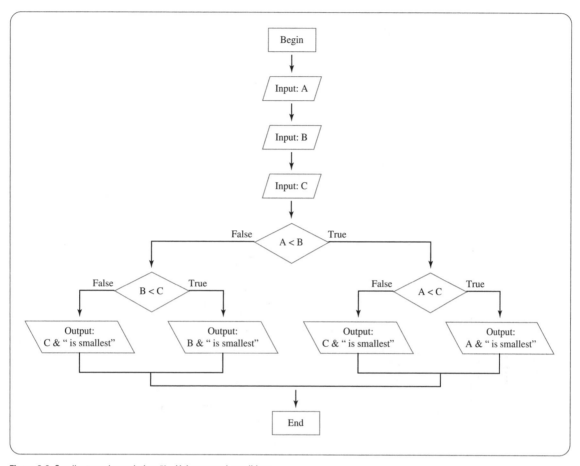

Figure 2-6 Smallest number solution #1 - Using nested conditions

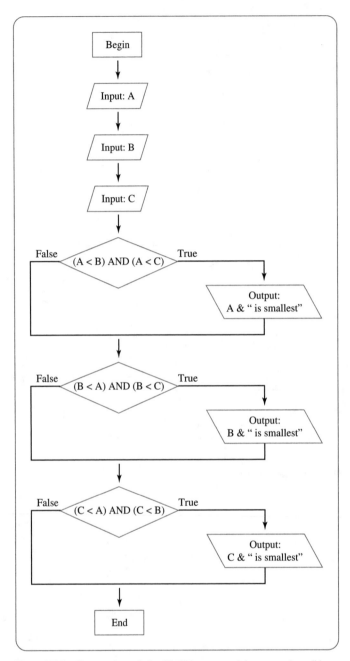

Figure 2-7 Smallest number solution #2 - Using sequential compound conditions

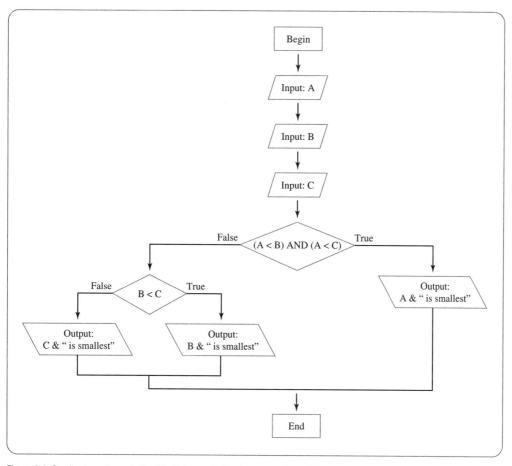

Figure 2-8 Smallest number solution #3 - Using nested and compound conditions

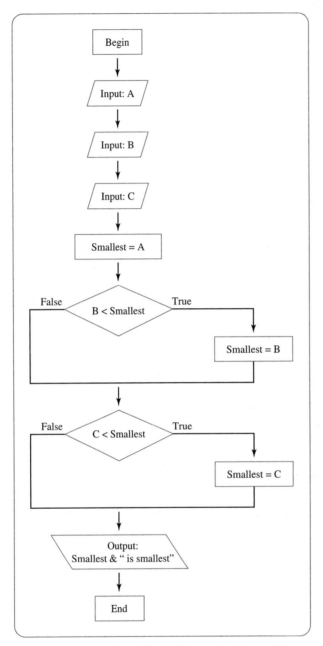

Figure 2-9 Smallest number solution #4 - Using a placeholder variable

CHAPTER SUMMARY

» A condition is an expression that evaluates to either true or false. Conditions typically use one of six relational operators: =, >, <, >=, <=, <>.

» IF statements use conditions to choose between actions. When executed, the condition is evaluated. If the condition is true, control flows to the true branch. If the condition is false, control flows to the false branch.

» The true and false branches of an IF statement may contain any valid statement, including other IF statements. An IF statement within the true or false branch of another IF statement is referred to as a nested IF.

» A compound condition is two or more conditions joined by a logical operator. The four most common logical operators are AND, OR, NOT, and XOR.

KEY TERMS

compound condition	IF statement	nested IF
condition	logical operators	relational operators

REVIEW QUESTIONS

1. What is the difference between a correct program solution and a good program solution? Why is it important for solutions to be not only correct but also good?

2. Identify possible uses of decision statements (IF statements) for a video store's rental checkout system.

3. The long-distance billing problem has a nested IF solution (Figure 2-4). This solution was rewritten as a compound condition solution (Figure 2-5). Can all nested IF solutions be rewritten as compound condition solutions? As part of your answer, consider the problem of inputting two values and displaying if the first is smaller than, equal to, or greater than the second (Figure 2-3). If it can be rewritten, include the new solution with your answer. If it cannot be rewritten, explain why not.

4. Consider the four solutions in Figures 2-6 through 2-9. These solutions assume the input data contains unduplicated numbers. Determine if each solution would work if duplicate input values were allowed (e.g., 3, 5, 3 as input).

PROGRAMMING EXERCISES

2-1. Positive Difference. Write a program that inputs two values and displays their positive difference. For example, if the first input is 6 and the second input is 9, then the positive difference is 3. Likewise, if the first input is 9 and the second input is 6, the output is still a positive 3.

Input Variable
Num1, Num2

2-2. All's Well That Ends Well. Write a program that inputs a number between 1 and 10 and displays the number with the appropriate two-letter ending (e.g., 1st, 2nd, 3rd, 4th, 5th, . . .).

> Input Variable
>
> Number

2-3. Middle Value. Write a program that displays the middle value of three unduplicated input values. *Hint*: Review the four solutions in the smallest number case study in this chapter. Consider how easy or hard it would be to modify each of those algorithms to find the middle value rather than the smallest value. Then modify the algorithm you consider most appropriate for this problem.

> Input Variable
>
> A, B, C

2-4. Smallest of Five. Write a program that displays the smallest of five input values that may include duplicate values (e.g., 6, 4, 8, 6, 7). *Hint*: Review the four solutions in the smallest number case study in this chapter. Consider how easy or hard it would be to modify each of those algorithms to find the smallest of five rather than three values. Then modify the algorithm you consider most appropriate for this problem.

> Input Variable
>
> A, B, C, D, E

2-5. Grade Determination. Write a program that will input three test scores. The program should determine and display their average. The program should then display the appropriate letter grade based on the average. The letter grade should be determined using a standard 10-point scale (A = 90–100; B = 80–89.999; C = 70–79.999, etc.)

> Input Variable
>
> Score1, Score2, Score3

2-6. All's Well That Ends Well, Part II. Write a program that inputs a number between 1 and 1000 and displays the number with the appropriate two-letter ending (e.g., 1st, 2nd, 3rd, 4th, 5th, . . .). *Hint*: This problem is harder than it sounds. The most common ending is th, but there are many exceptions. You might want to start by finding all the exceptions and looking for patterns. You might then find integer division (\) and integer remainder (Mod) helpful in testing for those patterns.

> Input Variable
>
> Number

2-7. The Perfect Fit. Write a program with three input variables, RW (for rectangle width), RH (for rectangle height), and SS (for square side). The program should output two sentences. The first sentence will be one of the following.

> "The object with the greatest area is the square."

> "The object with the greatest area is the rectangle."

> "The square and the rectangle have the same area."

The second sentence will be one of the following.

> "The square fits inside the rectangle."

> "The rectangle fits inside the square."

> "Neither shape fits inside the other."

Note: A 5 × 3 rectangle does not fit inside a 5 × 5 square; however, a 4.9 × 3 rectangle does fit inside a 5 × 5 square.

Input Variable	Process/Output Variable
RW, RH, SS	*(two sentences)*

WHILE LOOPS

CONSOLE INPUT AND OUTPUT

Sometimes you may want the input and output interactions with the user to be maintained for later inspection. This can be done through the use of **console** input and output statements. Figure 3-1 shows the input edit dialog window with the console input option button selected. (Click the "More >>" button to show the Console option button. A similar console option exists inside the output edit dialog window.) Figure 3-1 also shows a prompt to the user. This prompt will be used in place of the default prompt.

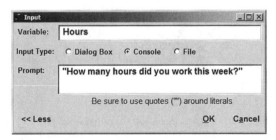

Figure 3-1 Input edit dialog window with the Console input option selected

The flowchart elements for console input and output have a console screen icon at the top of the flowchart element (see Figure 3-2).

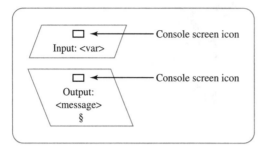

Figure 3-2 Console Input and Output elements

Console I/O is persistent, meaning each line of input and output remains in the console window for the lifetime of the program. The programs in Figure 3-3 illustrate the differences between Dialog I/O and Console I/O.

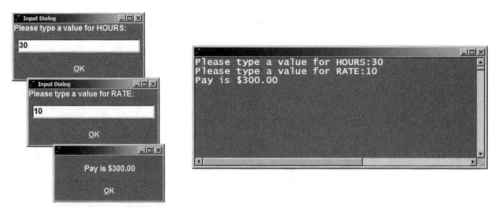

Figure 3-3 Dialog I/O (left) versus Console I/O (right)

>> **TIP** When you run a Visual Logic program that uses the console window, Visual Logic creates a second task in the Taskbar (at the bottom of your desktop). The console window may be hidden behind other open windows, so you may have to click on the second task to bring the console window to the front.

CONSOLE END-OF-OUTPUT CHARACTER

Because console output is persistent, multiple outputs can appear on the same line. The ending position of the current output (and therefore the starting position of the next console I/O) is indicated with the **end-of-output symbol (§)**. Figure 3-4 illustrates how the end-of-output symbol determines the starting location of the *next* line of I/O.

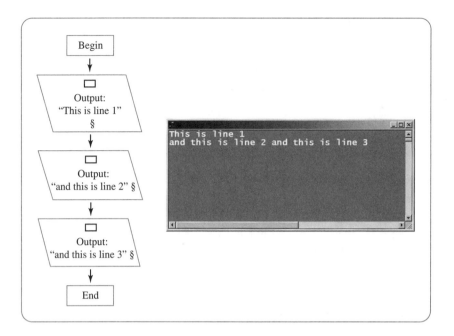

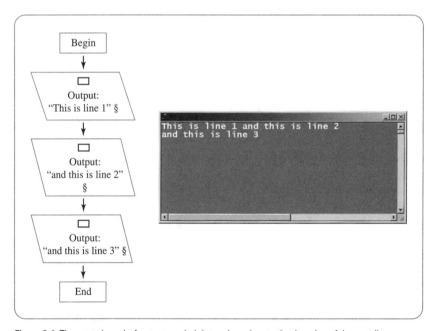

Figure 3-4 The console end-of-output symbol determines the starting location of the next line of console input or output

CONSOLE INPUT/OUTPUT SUMMARY

» Console I/O is persistent, meaning each line of input and output remains in the console window for the lifetime of the program.

» In Visual Logic, console input and output options are under the "More >>" button in the edit dialog, and console I/O is indicated by the presence of the console screen icon at the top of the flowchart element.

» The end-of-output (§) symbol always appears at the end of the console output expression. The position of the end-of-output symbol determines the starting location for the next console I/O.

WHILE LOOPS

While loops are used to repeat actions. As long as the condition inside the loop element evaluates to True, the body of the loop is executed and then control returns to the condition to be tested again. When the condition evaluates to False, the loop is complete and control flows to the element after the loop.

Figure 3-5 shows a common template for a While loop. In this example there is a **Loop Control Variable** (LCV) that is initialized before the loop begins, tested as part of the loop condition and updated as the last step inside the body of the loop.

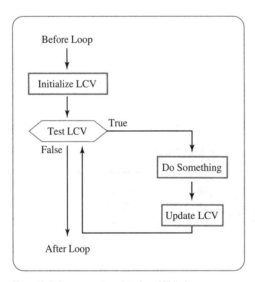

Figure 3-5 A common template for a While loop

A simple counting loop is shown in Figure 3-6. The variable "Count" is the Loop Control Variable, and it is initialized to 1, tested if less than or equal to 5, and updated by 1 each pass through the loop body.

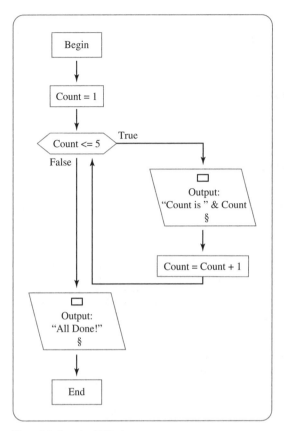

Figure 3-6 Counting While loop

Create the program shown in Figure 3-6 and then press F5 to run the program.

The initialization statement assigns the value 1 to Count. The program then flows into the Loop Test, which evaluates if Count <= 5. It evaluates to True and control flows into the body of the loop, generating the output:

Count is 1

The Count variable is updated (becoming 2) and the control flows back to the Loop Test. Because Count is still less than 5, the body of the loop executes again, generating the output:

Count is 2

This process of executing the body and then updating the loop variable repeats three more times, generating the following output:

Count is 3
Count is 4
Count is 5

After the fifth pass the loop variable is updated to the value 6. Because the loop variable is now greater than the final value, the loop is finished, and control leaves the loop and moves to the next element, which displays the message "Loop finished." Notice that console input and output are used, creating a record of I/O activity in the console window as shown in Figure 3-7.

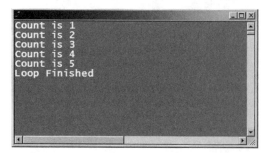

Figure 3-7 Output from program shown in Figure 3-6

>> **TIP** An **infinite loop** is what you get if there is no way for the loop to end. For example, if the "Count = Count + 1" statement was removed from Figure 3-6, then the resulting loop would be an infinite loop because the variable Count would always remain its initial value of 1, never becoming > 5, which is necessary to end the loop. (If you accidentally write an infinite loop when using Visual Logic, you can click the Terminate button on the toolbar or select Terminate from the Debug menu.)

Loops are simple but powerful ideas. Consider what happens when we slightly modify the program in Figure 3-6 by changing the condition and the output statements as shown in Figure 3-8. The resulting output, shown in Figure 3-9, seems much more complex but in fact the flowchart still follows the same simple design.

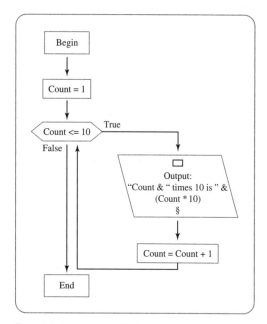

Figure 3-8 Another simple While loop

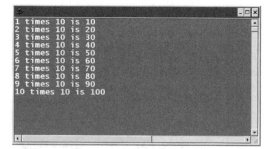

Figure 3-9 Output generated by Figure 3-8

PROGRAM: COUNTING BACKWARDS

Let's get more practice with While loops by solving the following problem:

Write a program that uses only one loop to print the even numbers from 60 down to 20, except for the value 40, which does not print, but instead two # symbols are printed in its place (e.g., 60, 58, 56. , . . . , 42, ##, 38, . . . , 24, 22, 20).

A first attempt to solve this problem is shown in Figure 3-10, which starts by setting the loop variable to an initial value of 60 and decrementing the loop variable by 1. Each time through the body of the loop, the loop variable is tested to see if it is an even value using the condition "Number MOD 2 = 0", which is true for even values (e.g., values divisible by 2.) Finally, when an even value is found, it is tested against the value 40 and if so, the "##" are printed instead of the value. This solution works and the output is shown in Figure 3-11.

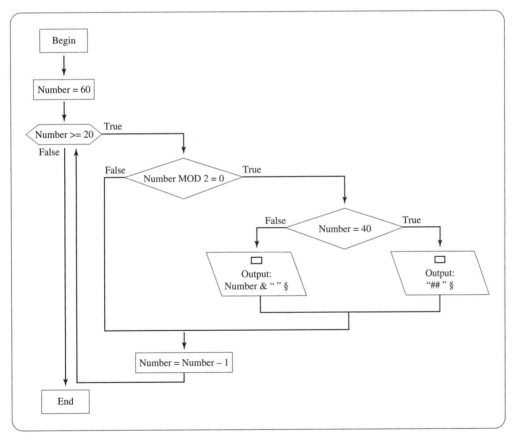

Figure 3-10 First solution for counting backwards problem

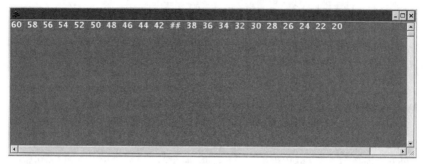

Figure 3-11 Output for counting backwards problem

A second, and better, solution to the counting backwards problem appears in Figure 3-12. In this solution the initial value is still 60, but the decrement is always -2. This eliminates the need to test for even values because the loop variable is always even. This is a simple change that makes the program much easier to read, while producing the same output (Figure 3-11).

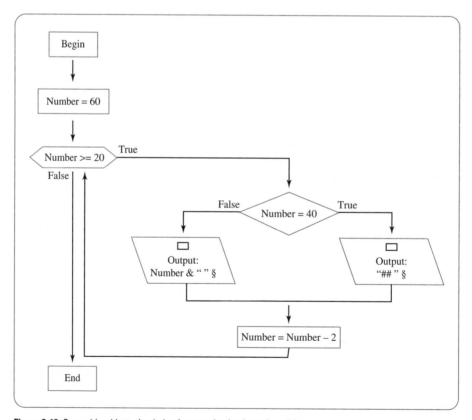

Figure 3-12 Second (and better) solution for counting backwards problem

QUICK CHECK 3-A

1. Use a While loop to display the squares of the numbers 1 to 10 (e.g., 1, 4, 9, 16, 25, etc.) in a console output window.

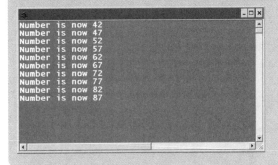

```
1 squared is 1
2 squared is 4
3 squared is 9
4 squared is 16
5 squared is 25
6 squared is 36
7 squared is 49
8 squared is 64
9 squared is 81
10 squared is 100
```

2. Use a While loop to display the numbers between 42 and 87 at intervals of 5 (e.g., 42, 47, 52, 57, etc.) in a console output window. (*Hint*: Use a statement like "Number = Number + 5" inside the body of your loop.)

```
Number is now 42
Number is now 47
Number is now 52
Number is now 57
Number is now 62
Number is now 67
Number is now 72
Number is now 77
Number is now 82
Number is now 87
```

WHILE LOOP SUMMARY

» While loops are used to repeat actions.

» In Visual Logic, the While loop flowchart element is a six-sided figure with a condition and two exit arrows, True and False.

» When control flows to the While loop, the condition is evaluated. If the condition is True, then control flows out through the True arrow into the body of the loop. At the end of the body of the loop the control flows back to the While loop and the condition is evaluated again. This process repeats until the condition eventually evaluates to False, at which time the control flows out through the False arrow to the statement after the While loop.

» When using the pre-test version of the While loop, the condition is tested first, and the loop body only executes if the initial test is true. When using the post-test version of the While loop, the loop body executes before the condition is tested; thus, the loop always executes at least one time. Both loops terminate when the condition evaluates to False.

WHILE LOOPS AND SENTINEL VALUES

There are many instances where you want to use a loop but you do not know how many times a loop will repeat. For example, a program that helps customers check out at a grocery store cannot assume how many items the person will have. One customer might have three items, and the next customer might have 42 items. It is necessary for the checkout program to work for both customers. A special value called a **sentinel value** (or signaling value) can be used to indicate all the data has been entered and the program should move on to the next phase of processing.

PROGRAM: GROCERY CHECKOUT REVISED

Consider again the grocery checkout program from Chapter 1. At that time we assumed the customer would purchase exactly three items, no more, no less.

An improved solution algorithm would be to allow the user to purchase as many items as desired. After the price of the last item is entered, a sentinel value is entered to indicate the end of input and to exit the loop. Sales tax would then be calculated and added to determine the total amount due. The solution flowchart for this algorithm is shown in Figure 3-13, and the program trace is shown in Figure 3-14.

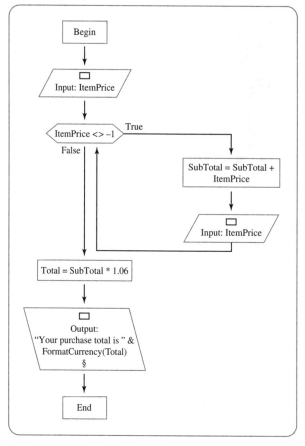

Figure 3-13 While loop with sentinel values used to solve grocery checkout problem

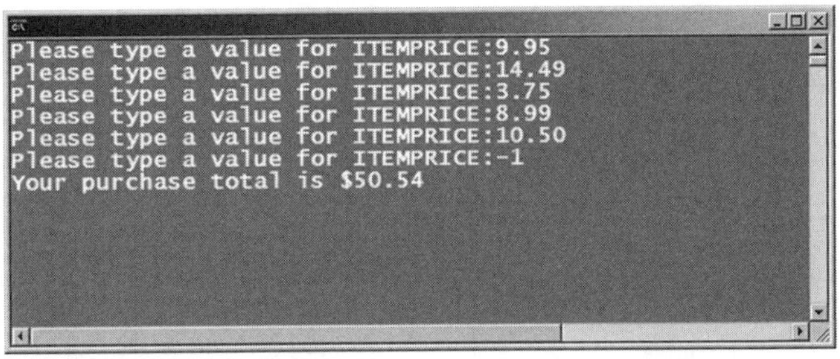

Figure 3-14 Output for Figure 3-13

> **>> TIP** The sentinel value can change from one program to the next. A sentinel value for a program should be a value that cannot be valid data. For example, negative one (–1) is a common sentinel value that works for many input types such as item price or exam scores, because –1 is not a valid price or exam score. (If something did cost negative one dollar, then you should buy a million of them and retire. Likewise, no matter how poorly a student does on an exam, the score will not be negative.) However, –1 is not a good sentinel value when working with weather temperatures because –1° Celsius is a valid temperature in many places around the globe. If the input is temperature values, then a good sentinel value might be 9999, which is well above the hottest weather temperature on Earth.

PROGRAM: DETERMINE THE AVERAGE

Let's get more practice with sentinel values by solving the following problem:

Write a program that reads a list of values terminated by the sentinel value −1. After the sentinel value is read, the program should display the average of the values entered (not including the sentinel value).

To calculate an average, you need to know two things: how many numbers are there and what is their total. Counter and accumulator variables can be used for this purpose. **Counters** are variables used to keep track of how many times a statement has executed. Counters update themselves by a constant value, typically 1. **Accumulators** are variables used to maintain a running total. Accumulators update themselves by the value of another variable or expression. Counters and accumulators are typically used inside the body of a loop to build up and maintain summary data on the information being processed. In Figure 3-15 the variable "Count" is a counter and the variable "Sum" is an accumulator.

Each time a non-sentinel value is read, that value is added to the Sum variable and the Count variable is updated by 1. After the sentinel value is entered, the loop finishes and the average is calculated based on the sum and count. (The sentinel value is not added or counted.) Figure 3-16 shows a sample run with three input values plus the sentinel value. Note that the sentinel value is not included in the count or the sum, and therefore is not part of the average.

Begin
Count = 0
Sum = 0
Input: Number
Number <> –1
True
False
Count = Count + 1
Sum = Sum + Number
Input: Number
Output:
"Count is " & Count
"Sum is " & Sum
"Average is " & (Sum/
Count)§
End

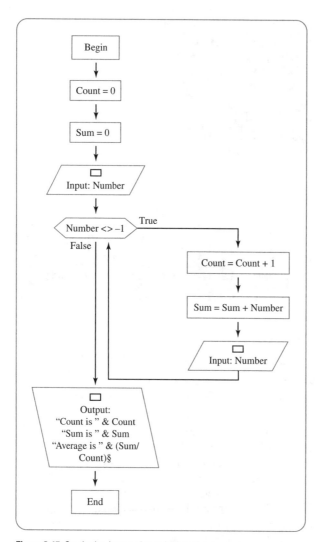

Figure 3-15 Sentinel value used to calculate the average

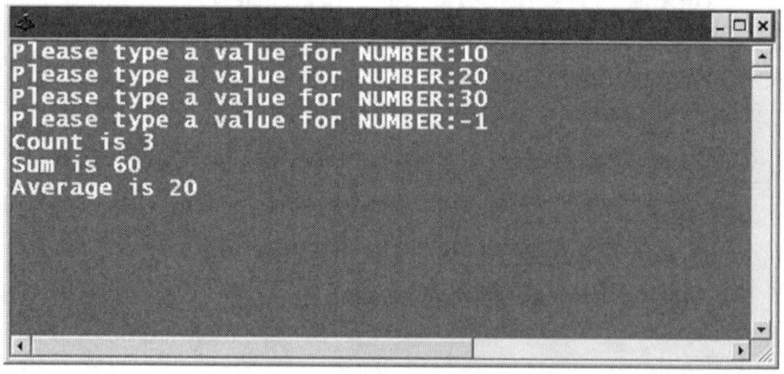

Please type a value for NUMBER:10
Please type a value for NUMBER:20
Please type a value for NUMBER:30
Please type a value for NUMBER:-1
Count is 3
Sum is 60
Average is 20

Figure 3-16 Output for Figure 3-15

>>> **TIP**
> Figure 3-15 includes the statements **Count=0** and **Sum=0** before those variables are used for counting and accumulation. While not required, it is common practice to initialize counters and accumulators directly above the loop where they are used.

SENTINEL VALUE, COUNTER, AND ACCUMULATOR SUMMARY

» Sentinel values are "end of data" values that indicate that all the data has been processed. Sentinel values are not part of the data set and should not be processed.

» Counters and accumulators are variables typically used inside a loop to help calculate counts, totals, and averages. Counters are typically incremented by one, and accumulators are typically updated by the value of a variable.

EXIT LOOP

An **Exit loop** causes control to jump out of the loop to the statement immediately below the loop. When using an Exit loop, the loop condition is typically set to the constant True, making sure the test always sends the control flow back into the body of the loop. The body of the loop begins with an input statement followed by a test to see if the input is the sentinel value. If so, then the Exit loop statement is executed, terminating the loop. If the input is not the sentinel value, then the remainder of the loop body is used to process the non-sentinel value. Figure 3-17 shows a template for a While loop with a sentinel input and an Exit loop.

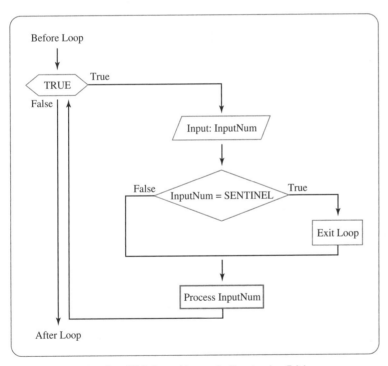

Figure 3-17 A template for a While loop with a sentinel input and an Exit loop

To illustrate how an Exit loop statement can be used, consider Figure 3-18 as a valid alternative to Figure 3-13. In this solution, the While loop condition is set to the constant True (so that the loop always repeats) and the first line in the loop body is the input statement. Immediately after inputting a value, the input is tested to see if it is the sentinel value. If it is, the Exit loop

>>TIP

The While loop condition should only be set to the constant "TRUE" when you are using an Exit loop inside the loop body; otherwise you will create an infinite loop.

statement is used to terminate the loop immediately. If the input is not the sentinel value, then the remainder of the loop body is executed to process the data in some appropriate manner. Both Figure 3-13 and Figure 3-18 produce exactly the same output, and there is no general consensus among developers about which sentinel solution is better. You are encouraged to understand both solutions.

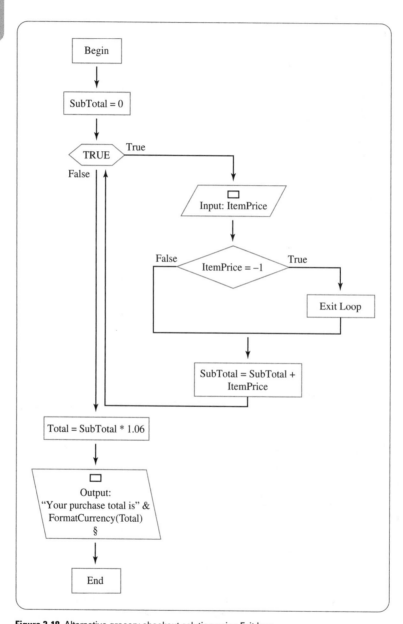

Figure 3-18 Alternative grocery checkout solution using Exit loop

PROGRAM: HIGH-LOW GAME

On the TV Show "The Price is Right" there is a game called "High-Low" where the contestant tries to guess a number (the price of an item) and the host tells the contestant "Higher" or "Lower" until the contestant guesses the number. We will now examine a program that plays a similar game. Rather than racing against the clock, the user will try to guess the number in the fewest number of guesses possible. Figure 3-19 shows a solution to this problem. A sample run of the program appears in Figure 3-20.

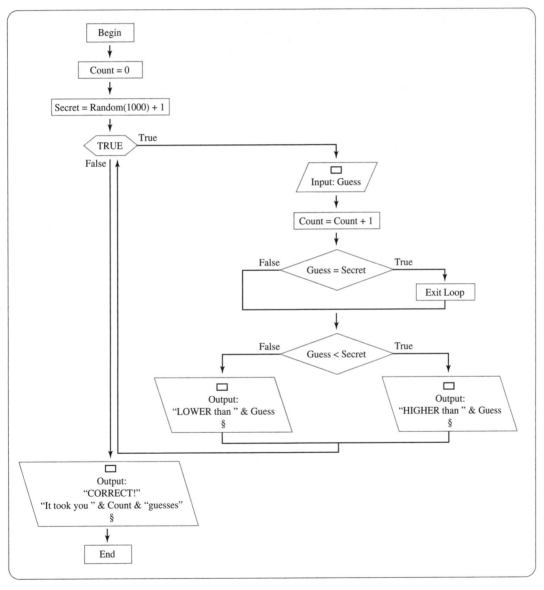

Figure 3-19 Solution to High-Low game

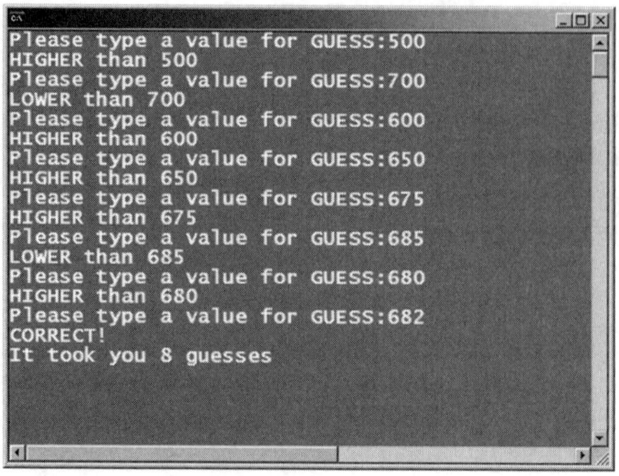

Figure 3-20 Sample run of Figure 3-19

EXIT LOOP SUMMARY

» The Exit loop statement causes control to jump directly to the statement following the current loop.

CHAPTER SUMMARY

» Console I/O is persistent, meaning each line of input and output remains in the console window for the lifetime of the program.

» In Visual Logic, console input and output options are under the "More >>" button in the edit dialog, and console I/O is indicated by the presence of the console screen icon at the top of the flowchart element.

» The end-of-output (§) symbol always appears at the end of the console output expression. The position of the end-of-output symbol determines the starting location for the next console I/O.

» While loops are used to repeat actions.

» In Visual Logic, the While loop flowchart element is a six-sided figure with a condition and two exit arrows, True and False.

» When control flows to the While loop, the condition is evaluated. If the condition is True, then control flows out through the True arrow into the body of the loop. At the end of the body of the loop, the control flows back to the While loop and the condition is evaluated again. This process repeats until the condition eventually evaluates to False, at which time the control flows out through the False arrow to the statement after the While loop.

» When using the pre-test version of the While loop, the condition is tested first, and the loop body only executes if the initial test is true. When using the post-test version of the While loop, the loop body executes before the condition is tested; thus, the loop always executes at least one time. Both loops terminate when the condition evaluates to False.

» Sentinel values are "end of data" values that indicate that all the data has been processed. Sentinel values are not part of the data and should not be processed.

» Counters and accumulators are variables typically used inside a loop to help calculate counts, totals, and averages. Counters are typically incremented by one, and accumulators are typically updated by the value of a variable.

» The Exit loop statement causes control to jump directly to the statement following the current loop.

KEY TERMS

accumulator	counter	Loop Control Variable (LCV)
console input	end-of-output symbol (§)	sentinel value
console output	Exit loop	While loop

REVIEW QUESTIONS

1. What are the three things that happen to a Loop Control Variable (LCV) in a simple While loop?

2. What is the difference between an accumulator variable and a counter variable?

3. What is the difference between a While loop with a pre-test and a While loop with a post-test?

4. Consider the solution to the High-Low game shown in Figure 3-19. If the assignment statement **Secret = Random(1000) + 1** was moved into the body of the loop, would the solution still work correctly? Why or why not?

5. Consider the solution to the High-Low game shown in Figure 3-19. If the assignment statement **Count** = **Count** + **1** was moved to the False branch of the "Guess = Secret" condition, would the solution still work correctly? Why or why not?

6. Consider the solution to the High-Low game shown in Figure 3-19. If the assignment statement **Count** = **Count** + **1** was moved to the bottom of the loop body, would the solution still work correctly? Why or why not?

PROGRAMMING EXERCISES

3-1. Merry Christmas. Write a program that uses a While loop to display "Ho Ho Ho Merry Christmas" to console output. *Note*: Your program should use the word "Ho" only once.

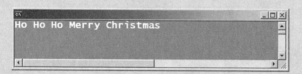

3-2. Cubed. Write a program that uses a While loop to display the cubes of the numbers 1 to 10 to console output.

```
1 cubed is 1
2 cubed is 8
3 cubed is 27
4 cubed is 64
5 cubed is 125
6 cubed is 216
7 cubed is 343
8 cubed is 512
9 cubed is 729
10 cubed is 1000
```

3-3. I'll Raise You Ten. Write a program that uses a While loop to display the value of 10 raised to the power of X where X is 1 through 5. (*Hint*: You can use the intrinsic function Power as part of your solution. Power(10,3) returns the value 1000.)

```
10 to the power of 1 is 10
10 to the power of 2 is 100
10 to the power of 3 is 1000
10 to the power of 4 is 10000
10 to the power of 5 is 100000
```

3-4. Four by Four. Write a program that uses a While loop to display the numbers between 37 and 77 at intervals of 4 (e.g., 37, 41, 45, 49, etc.) to console output.

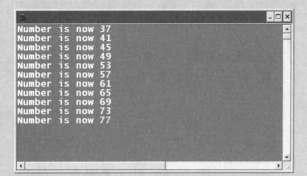

```
Number is now 37
Number is now 41
Number is now 45
Number is now 49
Number is now 53
Number is now 57
Number is now 61
Number is now 65
Number is now 69
Number is now 73
Number is now 77
```

3-5. Please Try Again. Write a program that asks the user to respond to a question by entering either 1 for yes or 2 for no. Use a While loop to continue prompting the user until a valid response is entered. Upon entering a valid response, the program should display an appropriate message to the user.

```
Are you happy? (1=yes, 2=no) 5
Please try again. Are you happy? (1=yes, 2=no) "Hello"
Please try again. Are you happy? (1=yes, 2=no) -1
Please try again. Are you happy? (1=yes, 2=no) 2
I'm sorry to hear that
```

3-6. Even-Odd Average. Write a program that reads a list of values from the user until the user enters the sentinel value –1. The program should then calculate and display the average of the even input values and the average of the odd input values, not including the sentinel. (*Hint*: Use two counters and two accumulators.)

```
Please type a value for NUMBER:20
Please type a value for NUMBER:30
Please type a value for NUMBER:55
Please type a value for NUMBER:77
Please type a value for NUMBER:-1
Even Average = 25
Odd Average = 66
```

3-7. King of the Hill. Write a program that reads in a list of positive integers from the user until the user enters the value −1 as a sentinel. At that time the program should display the largest value in the input list.

```
Please type a value for NUM:45
Please type a value for NUM:41
Please type a value for NUM:51
Please type a value for NUM:54
Please type a value for NUM:53
Please type a value for NUM:38
Please type a value for NUM:-1
Largest value was 54
```

3-8. Payment Plan. You have been hired to work for 10 days and you are given two payment options. The first option is to get paid $100 the first day and have your daily total increase by $100 each day. The second option is to get paid $2 the first day and have your daily total double each day. Write a program that determines your Day 10 payment for both options.

```
Day 1 Results: Plan1 = $100.00 and Plan2 = $2.00
Day 2 Results: Plan1 = $200.00 and Plan2 = $4.00
Day 3 Results: Plan1 = $300.00 and Plan2 = $8.00
Day 4 Results: Plan1 = $400.00 and Plan2 = $16.00
Day 5 Results: Plan1 = $500.00 and Plan2 = $32.00
Day 6 Results: Plan1 = $600.00 and Plan2 = $64.00
Day 7 Results: Plan1 = $700.00 and Plan2 = $128.00
Day 8 Results: Plan1 = $800.00 and Plan2 = $256.00
Day 9 Results: Plan1 = $900.00 and Plan2 = $512.00
Day 10 Results: Plan1 = $1,000.00 and Plan2 = $1,024.00
```

3-9. High-Low Redux. Write a solution to the High-Low game problem without using the Exit loop statement.

```
Please type a value for GUESS:500
HIGHER than 500
Please type a value for GUESS:700
LOWER than 700
Please type a value for GUESS:600
HIGHER than 600
Please type a value for GUESS:650
HIGHER than 650
Please type a value for GUESS:675
HIGHER than 675
Please type a value for GUESS:685
LOWER than 685
Please type a value for GUESS:680
HIGHER than 680
Please type a value for GUESS:682
CORRECT!
It took you 8 guesses
```

3-10. Account Balancer. Write a Visual Logic program to help balance a customer's bank account. The program should read numeric values that represent banking transactions. Special sentinel values will be read to indicate display-current-balance (8888) and end-of-the-month (9999) activities. In addition, the program solution should conform to the following requirements:

» The first value read is the starting balance.

» The program will then read integer values one at a time until the end-of-the-month sentinel value (9999) is read.

» Negative numbers are **checks** that reduce the account balance.

» Positive numbers (except for sentinel values) are **deposits** that add to the account balance.

» Any time a check is processed and the resulting balance is negative, the check bounces and there is a $10 fee assessed to the account (e.g., the balance is reduced by an additional 10 dollars).

» When the user inputs the special (sentinel) value 8888, the program should NOT treat this as a deposit, but instead should display the current account balance with a message formatted similar to:

```
The current balance is ####
```

» When the user inputs the special (sentinel) value 9999, the program should NOT treat this as a deposit, but instead should calculate the monthly service fee, which is either $10 or 10 percent of the account balance, whichever is smaller. Then the program should display the monthly service fee and the end-of-the-month balance with two messages formatted similar to the following lines:

```
The monthly service fee is ####
The account balance at the end of the month is ####
```

» The program ends after displaying the end-of-the-month account balance.

Two sample runs are shown below:

```
Please type a value for BALANCE:300
Please type a value for AMOUNT:500
Please type a value for AMOUNT:400
Please type a value for AMOUNT:9999

The monthly service fee is $10.00

The account balance at the end of the month is $1,190.00
```

```
Please type a value for BALANCE:100
Please type a value for AMOUNT:-50
Please type a value for AMOUNT:-30
Please type a value for AMOUNT:8888
The current balance is $20.00

Please type a value for AMOUNT:-40
Please type a value for AMOUNT:70
Please type a value for AMOUNT:8888
The current balance is $40.00

Please type a value for AMOUNT:20
Please type a value for AMOUNT:-30
Please type a value for AMOUNT:9999

The monthly service fee is $3.00

The account balance at the end of the month is $27.00
```

FOR LOOPS AND NESTED LOOPS

FOR LOOPS

For loops are used to automate the initialize, test, and update process. The best way to understand how For loops work is to look at a simple example. Start a new solution and add a For loop element from the element menu. Double-click the element to open the For Loop edit dialog window. Enter the following values (as shown in Figure 4-1): variable name **Count**; initial value **1**; final value **5**; and step **1**.

Figure 4-1 For Loop dialog window

Click OK to close the edit dialog box, and then add the two output statements as shown in Figure 4-2. Run the program and you will get the output shown in Figure 4-3.

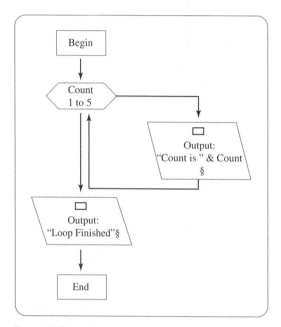

Figure 4-2 Simple For loop program

Figure 4-3 Output from program shown in Figure 4-2

COMPARING WHILE LOOPS AND FOR LOOPS

You probably recognize that there are numerous similarities between the While loop introduced last chapter and the For loop. Figure 4-4 shows a side-by-side comparison of two equivalent While and For loops.

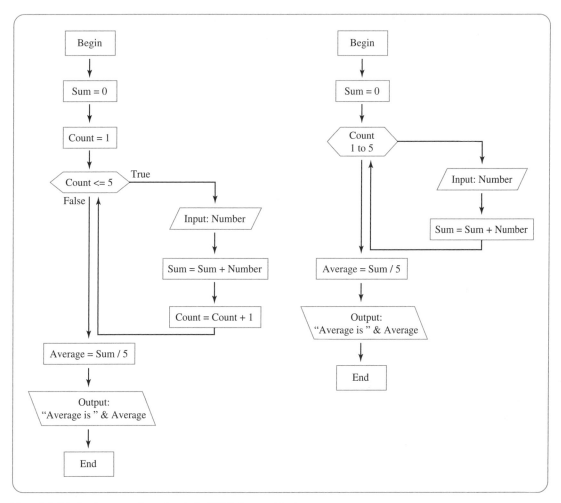

Figure 4-4 Side-by-side comparison of equivalent While Loop and For Loop

In the While loop version of Figure 4-4, there is an explicit initialization statement that sets the "Count = 1", an explicit test condition to test if "Count <= 5", and an explicit update statement inside the loop that sets "Count = Count + 1". The For loop performs these three actions (initialize, test, update) automatically based on the loop's ***initial value***, ***final value***, and ***step value***. When control first flows to the For loop, the loop variable is assigned the initial value. The For loop then repeats the body of the loop as long as the loop variable is less than or equal to the final value. Each time the body of the loop is executed, the For loop automatically updates the loop variable by adding the step value, and the process repeats.

> **»TIP**
> As Figure 4-4 illustrates, a For loop can be easier to read and understand than an equivalent While loop.

WORKING WITH FINAL AND STEP VALUES

Figure 4-5 shows a program with a step value equal to 5. The output for this program appears in Figure 4-6. The loop variable starts with the value 42 and increments by 5 after each pass through the loop (e.g., 42, 47, 52, 57, 62). After the fifth pass through the loop, the loop variable is incremented and becomes 67. Because the value of the loop variable now exceeds the loop's "final value" of 66, the loop terminates. This illustrates an important point, which is that the loop variable does not have to exactly match the final value, but rather that the final value is a threshold that, when crossed, terminates the loop.

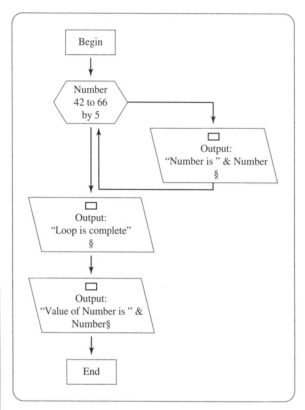

»TIP
The Visual Logic flowchart element for a For Loop does not show the step value when the step value is 1. When the step value is something other than 1, it will also appear in the flowchart element.

Figure 4-5 For Loop with step value equal to 5

```
Number is 42
Number is 47
Number is 52
Number is 57
Number is 62
Loop is complete
Value of Number is 67
```

Figure 4-6 Output generated by program in Figure 4-5

Figure 4-7 shows a For loop with a negative step value. When the step value is negative, the loop continues until the loop variable becomes smaller than the final value. The loop variable N has an initial value of 16 and is decremented by 2 after each pass through the loop until it exceeds (falls below) the final value of 4. Therefore the loop variable has the values 16, 14, 12, 10, 8, 6, and 4. The sum of those numbers is 70.

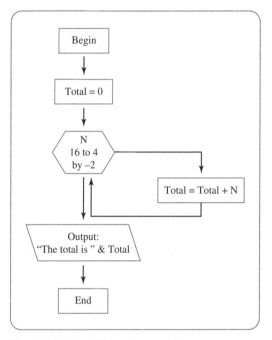

Figure 4-7 For loop with negative step value

Figure 4-8 Dialog output generated by program in Figure 4-7

FOR LOOP SUMMARY

» For loops are used to automate the initialize, test, and update process.

» In Visual Logic, the For loop flowchart element appears as a six-sided figure with a loop variable, a start value, an end value, and two exit arrows. (The step value also appears if the step value is something other than 1.) The body of the loop is to the right and below the element.

» When executed, the first action is to initialize the loop variable to the start value.

» The body of the loop executes as long as the value of the loop variable does not exceed the final value. (*Note*: If the step value is negative, then the body of the loop executes as long as the value of the loop variable is not smaller than the final value.) After the body of the loop executes, the loop variable is updated by the step value, and the process is repeated.

NESTED LOOPS

For loops and While loops are similar in that any valid statements can occur inside the body of a loop, including input, assignment, output, conditions, and even other loops. A ***nested loop*** refers to a loop contained inside the body of another loop. Figure 4-9 shows two examples of nested loops. Figure 4-9(a) shows a For loop nested inside a While loop. Figure 4-9(b) shows a While loop nested inside a For loop. Both programs produce the same output, which is shown in Figure 4-10.

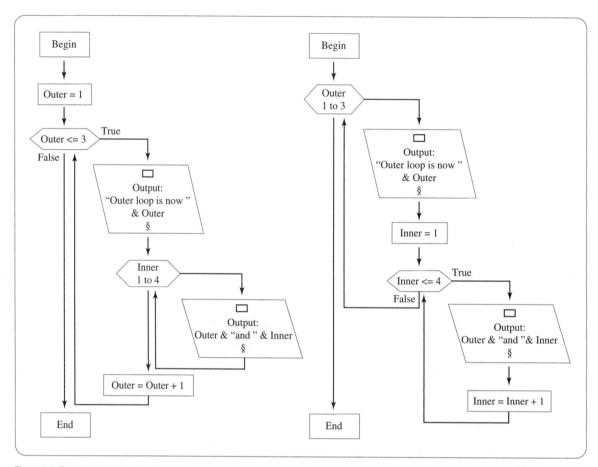

Figure 4-9 Two nested loop examples

```
Outer loop is now 1
1 and 1
1 and 2
1 and 3
1 and 4
Outer loop is now 2
2 and 1
2 and 2
2 and 3
2 and 4
Outer loop is now 3
3 and 1
3 and 2
3 and 3
3 and 4
```

Figure 4-10 Output generated by program in Figure 4-9

When working with nested loops, it is important to remember that the inner (nested) loop will be executed many times. Specifically, because the nested loop is part of the body of the outside loop, the nested loop executes in full each pass through the outside loop. Figure 4-11 shows three different programs that all have the same result, which is to display "Hello" 16 times.

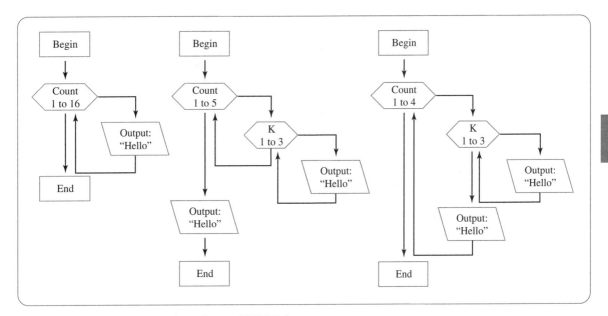

Figure 4-11 Three different programs that each output "Hello" 16 times

PROGRAM: MULTIPLICATION TABLE

Let's get more practice with nested loops by considering the problem of creating a multiplication table where each number in the table is the product of the row value multiplied by the column value. A 9 × 10 version of the table would look similar to the following:

```
 1  2  3  4  5  6  7  8  9
 2  4  6  8 10 12 14 16 18
 3  6  9 12 15 18 21 24 27
 4  8 12 16 20 24 28 32 36
 5 10 15 20 25 30 35 40 45
 6 12 18 24 30 36 42 48 54
 7 14 21 28 35 42 49 56 63
 8 16 24 32 40 48 56 64 72
 9 18 27 36 45 54 63 72 81
10 20 30 40 50 60 70 80 90
```

Figure 4-12 shows a solution for this problem. The left-hand line number is the value of a loop variable 1 to 10. Inside this loop there is a second loop that displays the nine values for that line. This inner loop therefore runs from 1 to 9. Each pass through the inner loop will multiply the row and column values and display the resulting product to console output. To help keep the output vertically aligned, we can add a test to see if the product is only a single digit and, if so, to print a leading space before displaying the number. Finally, after the inner loop completes and all nine values have been displayed on the same line, the program displays an output statement with the end-of-output character on the next line. This causes the console output to move to the next line in preparation for the next pass through the outer loop. The resulting output is shown in Figure 4-13.

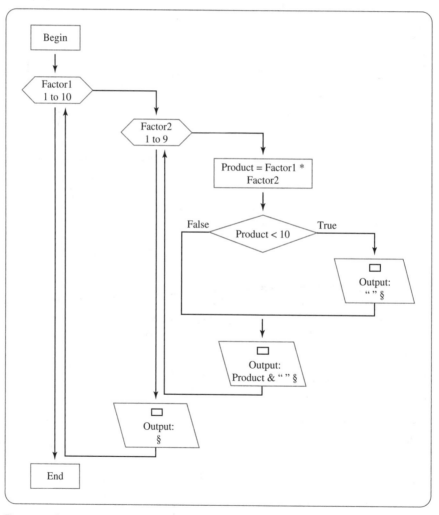

Figure 4-12 Solution to the multiplication table problem

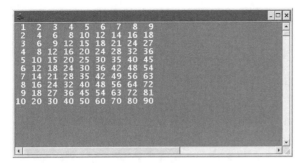

Figure 4-13 Output generated by the program in Figure 4-12

PROGRAM: TRIANGLE PROBLEM

Let's get more practice with nested loops by considering the problem of displaying a series of circles that form a right triangle like the following:

```
o
oo
ooo
oooo
ooooo
oooooo
ooooooo
oooooooo
ooooooooo
oooooooooo
```

This triangle has 10 lines of output. This suggests the solution should use a loop **LineCount** from 1 to 10 in which each pass through the loop generates one line of output.

When examining each line of output, we realize that each line contains the same number of circles as the line number (e.g., line four has four circles, line five has five circles, etc.). The solution therefore also has an inner loop **CircleCount** from 1 to **LineCount** for printing each line of circles.

Each horizontal line of circles can be generated by outputting one circle many times. This is done using a series of console output statements, each containing a single circle followed immediately by the end-of-output symbol (§). After the line is complete, an additional console output statement can be used to move the end-of-output symbol (§) to the beginning of the next line.

Figure 4-14 shows an implementation of the solution described above. Note that the nested CircleCount loop uses a variable, LineCount, as the final value, which causes the nested loop to have a different final value each time it is initialized. Also note that the output statement inside the nested loop prints one circle followed immediately by the end-of-output character on the same line. This causes the next circle to appear immediately after the previous circle. It is the output statement below the nested loop that moves the end-of-output character to a new line in preparation for the next line to begin (e.g., the next pass through the main LineCount loop.) The resulting output is shown in Figure 4-15.

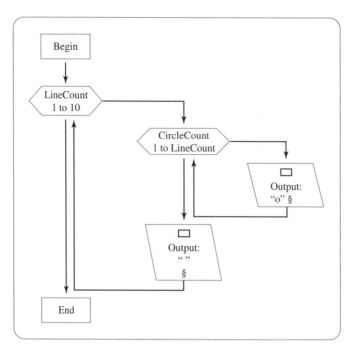

Figure 4-14 Solution to triangle problem

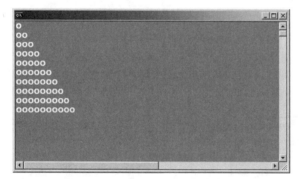

Figure 4-15 Output generated by program in Figure 4-14

NESTED LOOP SUMMARY

» Any valid statements can occur inside the body of a loop, including input, assignment, output, conditions, and even other loops.

» A nested loop refers to a loop that appears inside the body of another loop.

CHAPTER SUMMARY

» For loops are used to automate the initialize, test, and update process.

» In Visual Logic, the For loop flowchart element appears as a six-sided figure with a loop variable, a start value, an end value, and two exit arrows. (The step value also appears if the step value is something other than 1.) The body of the loop is to the right and below the element.

» When executed, the first action is to initialize the loop variable to the start value.

» The body of the loop executes as long as the value of the loop variable does not exceed the final value. (*Note*: If the step value is negative, then the body of the loop executes as long as the value of the loop variable is not smaller than the final value.) After the body of the loop executes, the loop variable is updated by the step value, and the process is repeated.

» Any valid statements can occur inside the body of a loop, including input, assignment, output, conditions, and even other loops.

» A nested loop refers to a loop that appears inside the body of another loop.

KEY TERMS

final value   initial value   step value

For loop   nested loop

REVIEW QUESTIONS

1. What is the difference between a For loop and a While loop?

2. When using a For loop, what happens when the loop variable is equal to the final value? What happens when the loop variable exceeds the final value?

3. Consider two For loops, one with a positive step value and one with a negative step value. How are these two loops similar? How are these two loops different?

4. When writing a program that reads input terminated by a sentinel value, which loop is more appropriate to use, a For loop or a While loop? Explain your answer.

5. Consider the following statement: "An infinite loop is more likely to occur when using a While loop than when using a For loop." Do you agree or disagree with the statement? Explain your answer.

PROGRAMMING EXERCISES

4-1. Blast Off! Write a program that uses a For loop to generate the output shown below. The text "Rocket launch" should appear only once in your program.

4-2. Pass It Around. Write a program that uses a For loop to generate the output shown below. Note that the program should only show the text for 99, 98, 97, and 96 bottles (*Hint*: Have a start value of 99 and a final value of 96, with a step value of –1).

```
99 bottles of rootbeer on the wall
99 bottles of rootbeer
Take one down and pass it around
One less bottle of rootbeer on the wall

98 bottles of rootbeer on the wall
98 bottles of rootbeer
Take one down and pass it around
One less bottle of rootbeer on the wall

97 bottles of rootbeer on the wall
97 bottles of rootbeer
Take one down and pass it around
One less bottle of rootbeer on the wall

96 bottles of rootbeer on the wall
96 bottles of rootbeer
Take one down and pass it around
One less bottle of rootbeer on the wall
```

4-3. Very Merry Christmas. Write a program that uses a nested loop to display "Ho Ho Ho Merry Christmas" five times to console output. *Note*: Your program should use the word "Ho" only once.

```
Ho Ho Ho Merry Christmas
Ho Ho Ho Merry Christmas
Ho Ho Ho Merry Christmas
Ho Ho Ho Merry Christmas
Ho Ho Ho Merry Christmas
```

4-4. Number Stack Different. Write a program that uses a nested loop to generate the output shown below. Be sure that the value on the line changes with each digit displayed. For example, line 5 has the values "1", "2", "3", "4", and "5".

```
1
1 2
1 2 3
1 2 3 4
1 2 3 4 5
1 2 3 4 5 6
1 2 3 4 5 6 7
1 2 3 4 5 6 7 8
1 2 3 4 5 6 7 8 9
```

4-5. Number Stack Same. Write a program that uses a nested loop to generate the output shown below. Be sure that all the values on a single line are the same. For example, line 5 has the values "5", "5", "5", "5", and "5".

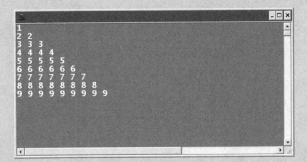

4-6. Right Triangle. Write a program that generates the following triangle to console output. Note that the number of blank spaces decreases each line. (*Hint*: Modify the solution in Figure 4-14 by adding a "SpaceCount" loop above the "CircleCount" loop. Both the SpaceCount and CircleCount loops should be nested inside the LineCount loop.)

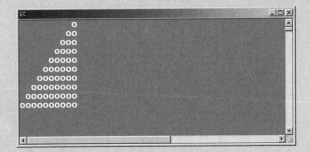

4-7. Tree. Write a program that generates the following tree shape to console output. Note that every line contains an odd number of circles.

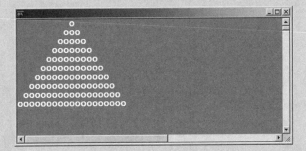

4-8. Diamond. Write a program that generates the following diamond shape to console output. Note that every line has an odd number of circles.

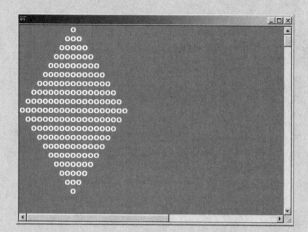

5

ARRAYS

Sorting Data

A dozen umbrellas lie on the ground just inside the classroom door when Dr. Taylor begins his lecture. "A cold, rainy day like today makes me want to stay in and order pizza for delivery rather than go out myself." Handing a phone book to a student in the front row, Dr. Taylor says, "Gail, please look up the phone number for Domino's Pizza on Main Street, and if you don't mind, I will time how long it takes you to find the number." Gail flips through a few pages while Dr. Taylor looks at his watch. "Here it is . . . 555-8275," she says.

"Seven seconds. Thank you Gail." Dr. Taylor presses some keys on his cell phone while continuing his conversation. "Now please look up the name of the person with the phone number 555-5982, and again I will time you." Dr. Taylor's focus returns to his watch even as he speaks into the phone. Gail slowly flips a couple of pages, then stops just about the same time Dr. Taylor ends his call. "I assure you the number is in there, Gail. We will wait while you look it up."

"You will probably wait a long time," she says, "because there is no fast way to find a number."

"Why not? It's the same data."

"But the phone book is sorted by names, so finding a name is easy. Finding a number is very difficult because a phone book is not sorted by numbers."

Dr. Taylor takes the phone book from Gail. "Exactly! The sorting process does not change the data, but it organizes the data in a context, making it useful information. Sorting is a fundamental processing activity, and we will discuss it very soon.

"But first, we need to discuss arrays, which are a useful means to hold large amounts of data, sorted or unsorted."

Dr. Taylor's sorting solution is presented later in this chapter.

ARRAYS

Sometimes it is beneficial to work with related data items as a single group. For example, all the scores from an entire class of students, all the names of employees for a company, or all the batting averages of the players on a baseball team. The easiest and most common way to store such related data is with an array.

An **array** is a variable that holds a collection of related data values. Each of the values in an array is called an **element**. Each element is like a separate variable, capable of storing and recalling a value as needed. Elements are uniquely identified by an integer value called its **index**, which indicates the position of the element in the array. The lowest index value is zero, and the largest index value is called the **upper bound**. Each element of an array is like a separate variable, capable of storing and recalling a value. To reference an element, you must specify both the array name and the specific index value.

CREATING AN ARRAY

In Visual Logic you create, or declare, an array using the **Make Array command**. The Make Array edit dialog contains text boxes for entering the name of the array and its upper bound. Figure 5-1 shows the Visual Logic Make Array dialog box for creating an array named "Scores" with an upper bound of 8. The resulting array is shown in Figure 5-2.

Figure 5-1 An example of the Make Array edit dialog box

Figure 5-2 The Scores array created by the Make Array command in Figure 5-1

ACCESSING INDIVIDUAL ELEMENTS OF AN ARRAY

To access individual array elements, you specify the array name and follow it with an index expression enclosed in parentheses. The value of the expression determines which element to access. The index to an array can be a constant, a variable, or an expression. For example, Scores(5) references the element with index value 5 in the array named Scores. Likewise, if K has the value 5, then Scores(K) also references the same element. Finally, if A is 2 and B is 3, then Scores(A + B) would also reference the index 5 element. Figure 5-3 includes a flowchart that creates an array and then assigns four values to that array. The resulting state of the array after the flowchart code is complete is also shown in Figure 5-3.

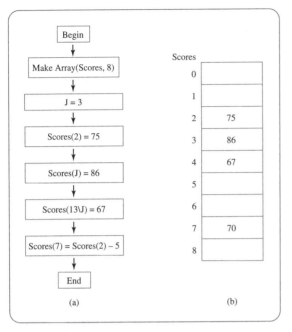

Figure 5-3 A flowchart with four array assignments and the resulting array elements

»TIP Arrays contain a finite number of elements, each of which is referenced by a unique index. If you attempt to reference an array with an index value greater than the upper bound of the array, the result will be an out-of-bounds error. For example, a reference to Scores(9) in the Figure 5-3 array would generate an out-of-bounds error because the index value 9 is greater than the upper bound for this array.

ARRAY SUMMARY

» An array is a storage location that holds a collection of related data.

» The values in the array are called the array elements.

» Individual elements in an array are identified by means of an index. Index values are integer values from 0 to the upper bound of the array.

» When referencing an element of an array, start with the array name and then specify the desired index inside parentheses.

» The index value that references an array can be provided by an integer constant, an integer variable, or an integer expression. This gives a great deal of power to developers when using arrays.

BENEFITS OF USING AN ARRAY

Arrays are valuable tools for developers. But what exactly is it about arrays that make them so helpful? One answer is that arrays combine the power of loops with the power of multiple storage locations. Consider briefly the following two problems:

(Problem #1) Input five numbers and output their average.

(Problem #2) Input five numbers and display the numbers in reverse order.

These two problems can both be solved without using arrays, but the two solutions will be very different. Figure 5-4 shows a common solution to both. The first problem would most likely be solved using a loop to minimize the inputs and allow the program to easily be modified to handle 50 or 500 inputs. The second problem requires five different storage locations and therefore a loop cannot be used. Furthermore, the second solution would be time consuming and monotonous to modify to handle 12 or 500 inputs.

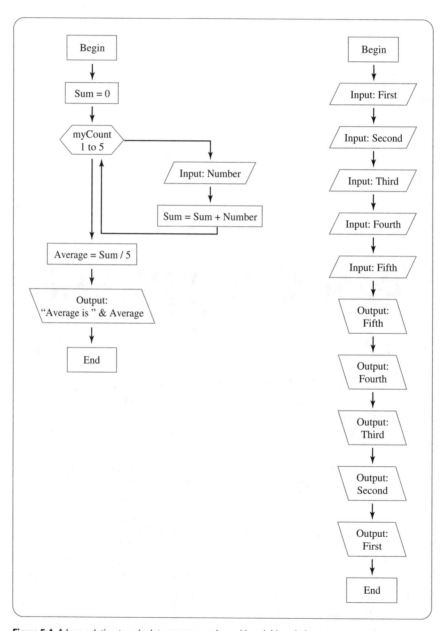

Figure 5-4 A loop solution to calculate average and a multi-variable solution to reverse order

The point of Figure 5-4 is to show that there are times when loops are desirable and there are times when separate storage locations are desirable. Now imagine a third problem that combines both of the previous problems. To make the problem even more interesting, assume there are 12 input values (rather than just five).

(Problem #3) Input 12 numbers and output their average and then display the input numbers in reverse order.

Neither solution in Figure 5-4 will solve this problem. (Take a few minutes if necessary to convince yourself that the previous statement is true.) However, this problem is easily solved using an array, as shown in Figure 5-5. The array solution combines the best features of the two programs from Figure 5-4, including having only a single input statement inside a loop, while also storing all the input values in separate storage locations so nothing is lost.

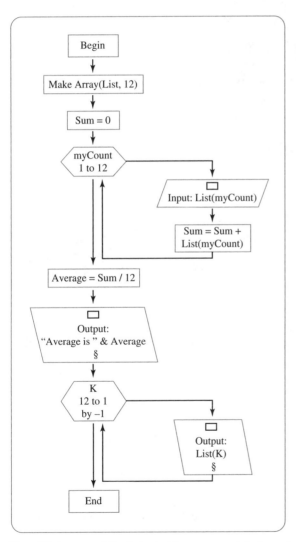

Figure 5-5 An array solution that calculates average and displays values in reverse order

When referencing an array inside the body of a loop, the loop variable is often used as the array's index value. As the loop variable changes from 1 to 2 to 3 to 4 (and so on), so also the array index changes from 1 to 2 to 3 to 4 (and so on). This allows the loop to process each element of the array.

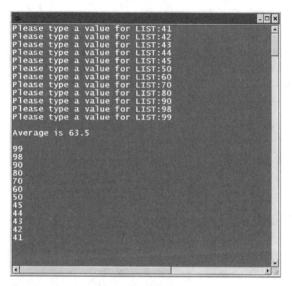

Figure 5-6 Sample output from Figure 5-5

>> **TIP** Many programs that utilize arrays will also employ For loops, with the For loop variable used as the index value for the array. Notice in Figure 5-5 that the first loop has the loop variable myCount and the first loop body uses myCount as the index value for the array in both the input and assignment statement. Then notice that the second loop has the loop variable K and the second loop body uses K as the index value for the array in the output statement. The general principle illustrated here is that when using a For loop to process an array, inside the body of that loop the For Loop variable is often used as the array index value.

BENEFITS OF USING AN ARRAY SUMMARY

» An array can be used to store multiple values in a single storage location. This makes the code easy to read and easy to work with.

» Arrays get their full power when used in conjunction with loops, where the body of the loop containing a reference to the array and the loop variable is used as the index value for the array.

SAMPLE PROGRAM #1: EVENS AND ODDS

Write a program that declares an array named List with an upper bound of 10. The program should prompt the user for 10 values and store them into the array. The program should then calculate and display the average of the 10 values. The program should then display the even values and their average, and the program should display the odd values and their average.

ANALYSIS AND DESIGN

Let's break this problem apart into separate requirements:

1. Write a program that declares an array named List with an upper bound of 10.

2. The program should prompt the user for 10 values and store them into the array.

3. The program should then calculate and display the average of the 10 values.

4. The program should then display the even values and their average.

5. The program should then display the odd values and their average.

Now that the problem has been broken into separate steps, these smaller pieces can be solved individually. Solving all the smaller pieces will therefore solve the larger problem. This technique is sometimes called "Divide and Conquer" and it works well for this problem. Figure 5-7 shows the solution to this problem, with the code for the individual requirements indicated.

The first requirement is satisfied by an appropriate Make Array command, being sure to use the required array name and upper bound value.

The second requirement is satisfied by an Input statement inside of a For loop. Note that the For loop variable, J, is used as the array index value List(J) in the Input statement.

The third requirement involves calculating an average, which means the program needs a total and a count. The count is known (it will be the average for all 10 values) and the total can be calculated inside a loop. Once the total has been generated, the average can be determined with a simple calculation.

The fourth requirement is to display the even values and their average. This requires a conditional test on each value in the array to see if the value is even (e.g., divisible by 2 with no remainder). If the value is even, it should be displayed, counted, and added to the appropriate total. After all even values have been found, the appropriate total and count values can be used to calculate and display the even average.

The fifth requirement is similar to the fourth and also requires testing each element in the array to see if the value is odd, and updating appropriate count and total values if so. After all odd values have been found and displayed, the appropriate count and total values are used to calculate and display the odd average.

By breaking the problem up into separate requirements and solving the individual pieces, we can solve the entire problem. Note that Figure 5-7 contains four loops and that the loop variable is different each time (J, K, M, N). Because these are not nested loops, we could have reused the same variable name each time. However, separate loop variables are used intentionally in Figure 5-7 to point out that the array index variable depends on the loop in which the statement appears. In other words, inside the K loop the array index is List(K), and inside the M loop the array index is List(M). Figure 5-8 shows the output generated by this program.

> **TIP** The idea of breaking a problem down into smaller parts and solving those smaller parts individually is one of the main reasons for the use of procedures, which is discussed in Chapter 6.

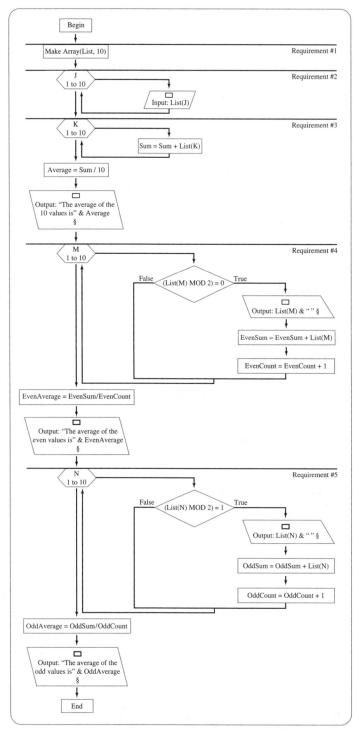

Figure 5-7 Solution to Sample Program #1: Even and Odds

Figure 5-8 Sample output from Figure 5-7

SAMPLE PROGRAM #2:
DICE ROLL SIMULATION

Computer simulations are powerful tools for studying the behavior of certain types of systems. In fact, today's engineer would never consider launching a satellite or producing a new automobile design without first creating computer simulations to model the product's behavior and functionality. While satellite and automobile performance simulations are beyond the scope of this book, a simple simulation such as rolling a single dice is something we can explore. Consider the following:

> *A single die is equally likely to roll a 1, 2, 3, 4, 5, or 6. While no single roll can be predicted, if the die is rolled many times, the roll values should move toward an even distribution. Specifically, as the number of rolls increases, the distributions should become closer to one-sixth, or 16.67%. Write a program that simulates rolling a single die many times. The program should maintain a count of how many times each of the six values was rolled. After all the rolls have been made, the program should display the totals of how many times each value was rolled.*

Write a program that performs a simulation of a single die rolled many times. The program should keep a running total of how many times each of the six values have been rolled. This running total should be kept in an array with an upper bound of 6. For example, every time the roll value is 3, the program should increment (or increase by 1) the value in the array at index 3. After the simulation is done rolling and counting, the program should display the total number of times each die value was rolled. Additionally, the program could present the simulation results in a visual manner as a histogram.

ANALYSIS AND DESIGN

This simulation requires a means to approximate the rolling of a die. This can be done using the expression **Random(6) + 1**. Random(6) produces a random integer between 0 and 5, and adding 1 to the result produces random values between 1 and 6, which is exactly what this simulation needs.

The problem also requires six different counter variables to keep up with how many times each of the six values was rolled. Using an array to hold the six counter values has the benefit that the random value can be used as the index of the array. In other words, Counters(5) holds a count of how many times 5 was rolled, and each time the random roll value is 5, the Counters(5) value is updated to be increased by 1.

Finally, after all the values have been rolled and counted, the program displays the totals and their percentages as well as a histogram of the data. The histogram is generated using nested loops. The inner loop generates a horizontal line of circles whose length is determined by the counter value (one circle for each time the die value was rolled). Following the loop to print the circles is an output with a carriage return to terminate the line. The outer loop then repeats the inner loop process for each of the six roll values.

The complete solution is shown in Figure 5-9. Two sample outputs with 400 rolls are presented in Figure 5-10. Each run will be slightly different because random values will generate different totals.

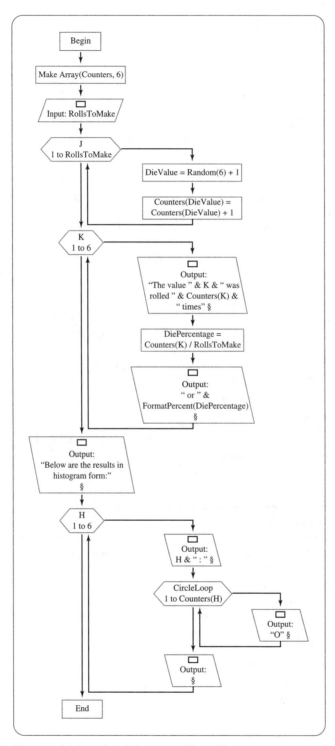

Figure 5-9 Solution to Sample Program #2: Dice Roll Solution

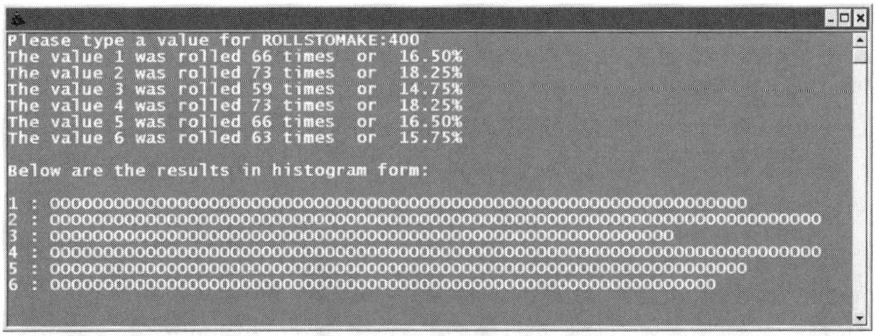

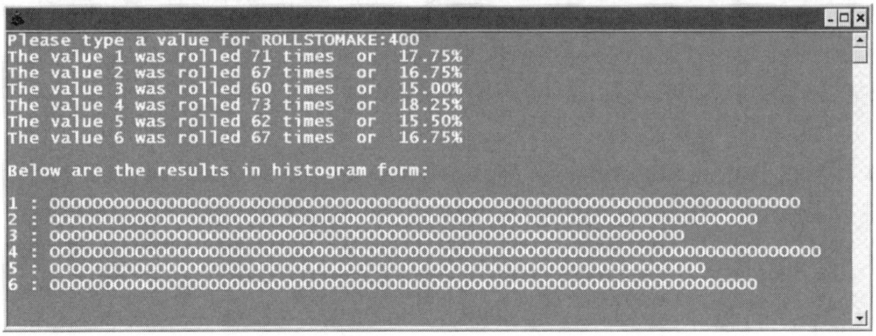

Figure 5-10 Sample outputs from running Figure 5-9 twice (Notice how the random values produce different results)

SAMPLE PROGRAM #3: PARALLEL ARRAYS (USERNAME AND PASSWORD)

In this section we examine a problem that involves maintaining two parallel arrays. The first array holds usernames and the second array holds passwords. The two arrays are separate but related, each having the same number of elements, and the values in one correspond to the values in the other. For example, the seventh element in the username array and the seventh element in the password array together form a valid username/password combination that would grant authentication to the system.

Write a program that reads 10 username and password pairs and stores those username and password values into parallel arrays. After the arrays have been loaded, the program should behave as a login screen, prompting for a username and a password. Based on the data entered for username and password, the program should respond appropriately with one of three output messages. If the username does not match one of the values in the username array, then the message should be *"Username not found."* If the username is found in the username array, but the password does not match the parallel value in the password array, then the message should be *"Username and password do not match."* If the username is found and the password matches the parallel value in the password array, the message should be *"Access granted."*

READING DATA FROM A TEXT FILE

In addition to Dialog and Console input, there is a third input option called File input, which allows the input data to come from a text file rather than being manually typed in each time the program is executed. In this program, for example, the 10 username and password pairs can be entered one time into a simple text file and those values can then be read from the text file into the parallel arrays each time the program is executed. This will eliminate redundant typing and reduce the likelihood of a typing error.

To perform file I/O, double-click on the Input (or Output) element to show the edit dialog, click "More >>", select the File option button, and then specify the appropriate text file name.

> **TIP** The authors have created a **usernames.txt** input file for this program, which may be made available to you, or your instructor may have created an input file for you to use. At the same time, you can create your own input file as well using Notepad or a similar tool to create a simple .txt file. When creating an input file, remember that each line in the file corresponds to one input value. You should therefore keep the input file to one input item per line, being sure to include quotes around string input, just like with console or dialog input.

Four tips to remember when doing file I/O:

1. First, when creating your input text file, DO use quotes around string data inside the text file. (Note that File input works the same as Console input in that strings must have delimiting quotes, and that the delimiters can be either single or double quotes, just so long as you use the same delimiter to start and stop the string.)

2. Second, do NOT use quotes around the text file name in the I/O dialog.

3. Third, if your file name in the I/O dialog box uses a relative reference (without the full path name), the text file needs to be in the same folder as the Visual Logic.exe executable (which is not necessarily the same folder as the *.vls solution file).

4. Fourth, if you have both FileInput and FileOutput in the same program, you must use different file names for the Input and Output files.

ASK THE AUTHOR

Q: Are usernames and passwords typically saved as text files?

A: No. (Thank goodness.) A text file with usernames and passwords would not be very secure and you certainly would not want your bank account information stored in this format. An enterprise system would most likely store username and password data in a password-protected database.

ANALYSIS AND DESIGN

We begin our implementation of the username and password solution by confirming that we have a valid text file with username and password pairs. Figure 5-11 shows the username and password pairs from the username.txt file. Note that the first four username and password pairs are "peanut butter"/"jelly," "sunrise"/"sunset," "light"/"dark," and "forward"/"reverse." Those values are read and stored into parallel arrays that will look like Figure 5-12.

Figure 5-11 Usernames.txt input file

Username				Password		
0				0		
1	"peanut butter"			1	"jelly"	
2	"sunrise"			2	"sunset"	
3	"light"			3	"dark"	
4	"forward"			4	"reverse"	
5	"water"			5	"oil"	
6	"burgundy"			6	"gold"	
7	"sofa"			7	"chair"	
8	"boy"			8	"girl"	
9	"fire"			9	"water"	
10	"build"			10	"destroy"	

Figure 5-12 Parallel arrays after reading data from input file

Once the parallel arrays have their data, the program prompts the user for a username. The program checks the user's input against the Username array, looking for a match. If the entire array is searched and no match is found, then the program gives the "Username not found" error message. If the username is found, the program prompts the user to input the associated password. The program then looks in the Password array at the same index value location where the Username was found. If the user-entered password matches the associated password in the parallel array, then the program gives the "Access granted" message; otherwise the program gives the "Username and password do not match" error message. The solution to this problem is shown in Figure 5-13, and three sample runs are shown in Figure 5-14.

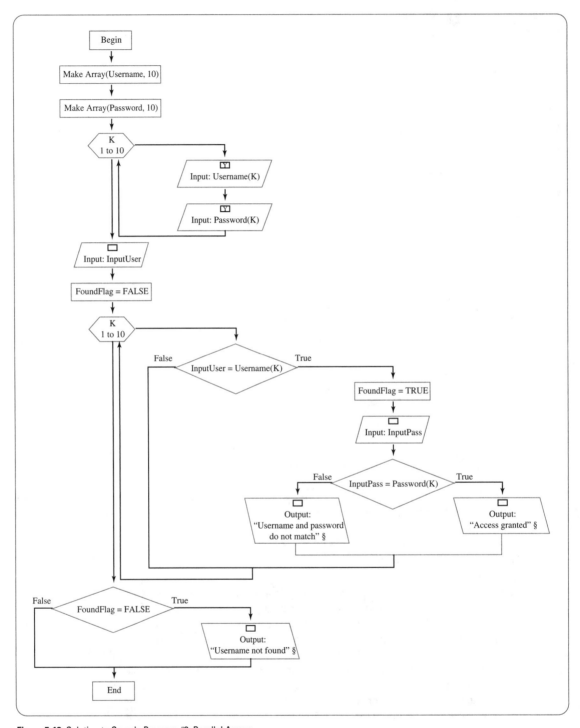

Figure 5-13 Solution to Sample Program #3: Parallel Arrays

```
Please type a value for USER:"yesterday"
Username not found
```

```
Please type a value for USER:"water"
Please type a value for PASS:"ice"
Username and password do not match
```

```
Please type a value for USER:"water"
Please type a value for PASS:"oil"
Access granted
```

Figure 5-14 Output from Figure 5-13

>> **CASE STUDY SOLUTION**

Sorting Data

"Probably the simplest way to sort an array is a technique called bubble sort. The basic idea is to repeatedly compare two adjacent values and swap them if they are in the wrong order. The bigger values flow in one direction, and the smaller values flow in the other direction." Dr. Taylor turns to the blackboard, draws an array with nine elements, and fills them with apparently random values.

"The heart of the solution is a loop from the start to the end of the array. The loop swaps adjacent elements if necessary as it goes. After one pass through the array, the largest value will have moved to the end of the array." Dr. Taylor makes a few marks on the chalkboard to illustrate the eight comparisons needed to pass through the entire array and the resulting location of the largest element in the final position (see Figure 5-15).

"If you repeat the loop a second time, the second largest element will be placed in its proper location." Dr. Taylor makes additional marks on the chalkboard to represent the second pass through the array (see Figure 5-16).

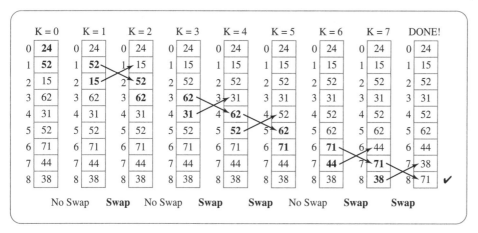

Figure 5-15 Array after one pass (one value guaranteed to be in proper location)

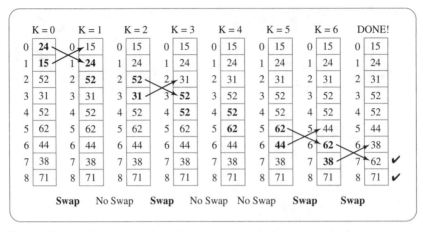

Figure 5-16 Array after two passes (two values guaranteed to be in proper locations)

Dr. Taylor continues, "After two passes, there are two elements that are certain to be in their proper locations. Three passes ensure three elements are in the proper location and so on. Sorting the array, therefore, requires N–1 passes where N is the number of elements in the array. If N–1 elements are in the proper location, the Nth element must also be in the proper location."

He then begins handing out a sheet with a solution similar to Figure 5-17 printed on it. "This handout shows a simple implementation of bubble sort. Notice the two loops we just discussed. The solution also includes code to display the sorted values." Figure 5-18 shows the output generated by the solution in Figure 5-17.

"Are there other sorting algorithms?" Leslie asks.

"Absolutely, and almost all of them run faster than bubble sort. But bubble sort is the easiest to understand, and it works fine with arrays of size 5,000 or less. If the size of the array is significantly bigger than that, you will probably need to consider one of the faster, more complex sorting algorithms."

A few more aspects of the bubble sort algorithm are discussed in the remaining few moments of the class. Finally, there is a knock on the classroom door by a Domino's delivery person holding a flat, cardboard box. Dr. Taylor smiles, as the aroma of pepperoni and sausage pizza fills the room. Glancing at his watch, he announces, "My lunch has arrived with perfect timing. Class dismissed."

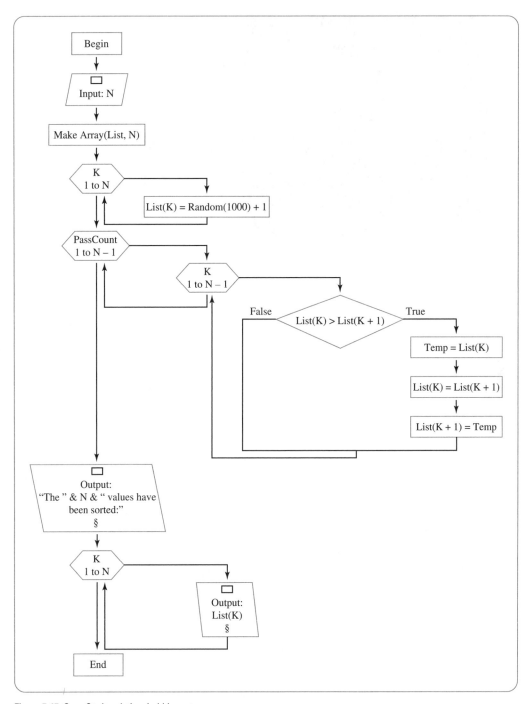

Figure 5-17 Case Study solution: bubble sort

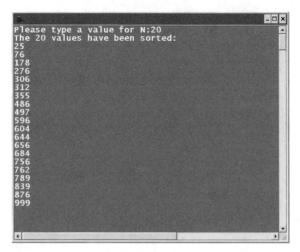

Figure 5-18 Sample output for Figure 5-17

CHAPTER SUMMARY

» An array is a variable that holds a collection of related data values. Each of the values in an array is called an element. Each element in the array is identified by an integer value called its index, which indicates the position of the element in the array.

» Most modern programming languages implement zero-based arrays, meaning that array index values begin with 0. The length of an array is the number of elements in the array. The upper bound of an array is the index of the last element.

» To access individual array elements, you specify the array name and follow it with an index expression enclosed in parentheses. The value of the expression determines which element to access.

» Arrays contain a finite number of elements, each of which is referenced by a unique index. If you attempt to reference an array with an index value greater than the upper bound of the array, the result will be an out-of-bounds error.

» Parallel arrays are two or more arrays whose elements are related by their positions in the arrays.

» Bubble sort is a simple sorting technique involving multiple passes through the array, each pass comparing adjacent elements and swapping them if necessary.

KEY TERMS

array	index	upper bound
array length	Make Array command	zero-based arrays
bubble sort	out-of-bounds error	
element	parallel arrays	

REVIEW QUESTIONS

1. How is an array with five elements similar to having five different variables?

2. How is an array with five elements better than having five different variables?

3. What is the difference between an array index and an array element?

4. What is the difference between an array length and an array upper bound?

5. In Visual Logic, how is an array declared?

6. The index value for an array can be a variable. Explain how this is helpful when writing programs.

7. Identify some general recommendations for when an array should be used.

8. Consider the bubble sort solution in Figure 5-17. What is the purpose of the Temp variable? Explain why swapping two values could not be done without a third storage location.

PROGRAMMING EXERCISES

5-1. Reverse. Write a program that uses an array to accept 10 input values and store them into an array. The program should then display those 10 numbers in reverse order.

```
Please type a value for LIST:10
Please type a value for LIST:20
Please type a value for LIST:30
Please type a value for LIST:31
Please type a value for LIST:32
Please type a value for LIST:33
Please type a value for LIST:34
Please type a value for LIST:35
Please type a value for LIST:40
Please type a value for LIST:50

The values in reverse order are:

50
40
35
34
33
32
31
30
20
10
```

5-2. Above Average. Write a program that accepts five input values and stores them into an array. The program should then display the average of the five numbers. Finally, the program should display all the numbers in the array that are larger than the average of the five numbers.

```
Please type a value for LIST:10
Please type a value for LIST:45
Please type a value for LIST:35
Please type a value for LIST:20
Please type a value for LIST:30

The average is 28

The following are greater than the average:
45
35
30
```

5-3. Target Value. Write a program that accepts 10 input values and stores them into an array. After reading the 10 values, the program should then input one more value, which is called the target value. The program should then search through the array to calculate and display how many times the target value appears inside the array.

```
Please type a value for LIST:7
Please type a value for LIST:7
Please type a value for LIST:4
Please type a value for LIST:5
Please type a value for LIST:3
Please type a value for LIST:2
Please type a value for LIST:3
Please type a value for LIST:7
Please type a value for LIST:5
Please type a value for LIST:7
Please type a value for TARGETVALUE:7

The target value appears 4 times in the array.
```

5-4. Batting Average. Write a program that uses parallel arrays to determine the batting average for a baseball team by position. There are nine positions on a baseball team and your program should have parallel arrays with an upper bound of 9. Your program will read data in pairs; the first number will be between 1 and 9 and will represent the batter's position, and the second number will be either 0 or 1 and will represent an out (0) or a hit (1). The program will continue to input data pairs until the sentinel value −1 is read. At that point, the program should output the batting average for each of the nine positions. (*Note*: Batting average is the number of hits divided by the number of at bats. Therefore, hits and at bats may be good values to store in parallel arrays.) The output shown below was generated using the input file "battingaverage.txt," which may be available from your instructor.

```
424 pairs of data were read from a file.

The batting average for each position was:
Position 1 batting average is 0.346938775510204
Position 2 batting average is 0.240740740740741
Position 3 batting average is 0.274509803921569
Position 4 batting average is 0.268292682926829
Position 5 batting average is 0.234042553191489
Position 6 batting average is 0.222222222222222
Position 7 batting average is 0.322033898305085
Position 8 batting average is 0.304347826086957
Position 9 batting average is 0.219512195121951
```

5-5. Batting Average and Slugging Percentage. Write a program that uses parallel arrays to determine the batting average and slugging percentage for a baseball team by position. There are nine positions on a baseball team and your program should have parallel arrays with an upper bound of 9. Your program will read data in pairs; the first number will be between 1 and 9 and will represent the batter's position, and the second number will be either a 0 (for an out) or a 1 (for a single) or a 2 (for a double) or a 3 (for a triple) or a 4 (for a home run). The program will continue to input data pairs until the sentinel value −1 is read. At that point, the program should output the batting average and slugging percentage for each of the nine positions. (*Note*: Batting average is the number of hits divided by the number of at bats and slugging percentage is the total number of bases divided by the number of at bats. You might want to have three parallel arrays in your solution.) The output shown below was generated using the input file "battingandslugging.txt," which may be available from your instructor. (*Hint*: You will probably need parallel arrays for Hits, AtBats, and Bases.)

```
424 pairs of data were read from a file.

The batting average for each position was:
Position 1 batting average is 0.346938775510204
Position 2 batting average is 0.240740740740741
Position 3 batting average is 0.274509803921569
Position 4 batting average is 0.268292682926829
Position 5 batting average is 0.234042553191489
Position 6 batting average is 0.222222222222222
Position 7 batting average is 0.322033898305085
Position 8 batting average is 0.304347826086957
Position 9 batting average is 0.219512195121951

The slugging percentage for each position was:
Position 1 batting average is 0.530612244897959
Position 2 batting average is 0.37037037037037
Position 3 batting average is 0.509803921568627
Position 4 batting average is 0.292682926829268
Position 5 batting average is 0.25531914893617
Position 6 batting average is 0.388888888888889
Position 7 batting average is 0.627118644067797
Position 8 batting average is 0.434782608695652
Position 9 batting average is 0.268292682926829
```

5-6. Two Dice Simulation. Write a program that simulates the rolling of two dice many times. Each of the two dice should have a separate "Random(6) + 1" and the two random values should be added together to get the total of the two dice roll. After rolling the two dice, the total rolled should be updated in an array of counters. For example, if the random values were 3 and 4, then the dice total is 7, and the index 7 element should be incremented by 1. Because the maximum roll possible for two dice is 12, your array of counters should have an upper bound of 12. Your program should simulate rolling the two dice many times (400 rolls is the number used in the figure below) and then display how many times each total was rolled and the percentage for each total. Finally, the program should display the roll totals visually by creating a histogram. *Note*: Each time you run your program you will get different totals and therefore a different histogram. In general the middle totals (such as 6, 7, 8) should be rolled more often than the extremes (2, 3, 4 on the low end and 10, 11, 12 on the high end) because there are more combinations of two dice that result in those middle values.

5-7. Access Granted. Write a program that reads 10 username and password pairs and stores those username and password values into parallel arrays. After the arrays have been loaded, the program should behave as a login screen, continuously prompting for a username and password until a valid combination is entered and access is granted. Each time the user enters username and password data, the program should respond appropriately with one of three output messages. If the username does not match one of the values in the username array, then the message should be *"Username not found."* If the username is found in the username array, but the password does not match the parallel value in the password array, then the message should be *"Username and password do not match."* If the username is found and the password matches the parallel value in the password array, the message should be *"Access granted."* The program should use a loop and continue to prompt the user for a valid username and password pair until a valid pair is entered and access is granted.

5-8. Olympic Judging. When judging an Olympic event, the highest and lowest judges' scores are often dropped, and the remaining judges' scores are averaged. Write a program that accepts six numeric values as input representing scores from six Olympic judges. The program should store those six values into an array. Your program should then use bubble sort to sort the scores in the array. Finally, your program should output the highest score, the lowest score, and the average of the other four scores.

```
Please type a value for SCORES:3
Please type a value for SCORES:2
Please type a value for SCORES:1
Please type a value for SCORES:4
Please type a value for SCORES:9
Please type a value for SCORES:5
Highest score : 9
Lowest score : 1
Olympic Average : 3.5
```

6

GRAPHICS AND PROCEDURES

Drawing Houses

"The materials we have covered so far in this course, including expressions, conditions, loops, and arrays are founda-
tional concepts essential to most any programming language," Dr. Taylor says at the beginning of class. "Visual Basic, C#,
C++, Java, Cobol, Pascal, and other popular languages all use these commands in their solutions. Even graphical languages
use these commands."

"What's a graphical language?" one student asks.

"Graphical languages contain graphics commands that allow developers to create programs that generate a variety of
interesting, pictorial outputs." Dr. Taylor turns on the overhead projector and shows a series of images, including geometric
figures and colorful designs. "For example, all these images were created with Visual Logic graphics commands combined with expressions, conditions, and loops."

Dr. Taylor walks away from the projector to the desk at the front of the room. "In addition to graphics, we will also discuss
a common strategy for solving complex problems, which is to break the problem down into smaller pieces, solve the smaller
pieces individually, and then put the pieces back together to solve the original problem."

"Kind of like divide-and-conquer?" asks Stephanie.

"Yes, exactly. We write solutions to the small pieces in blocks called procedures. We then call the procedures as necessary
to solve the original problem."

Jay raises his hand. "Did you say we will write programs that generate all those images?" he asks, pointing to the screen
that is still showing various graphics outputs.

"Yes. We will soon be making the images you see on the screen. That last image, the one with multiple houses, requires
both graphics and procedures. But we start with simple geometric shapes."

Dr. Taylor's solution to the house graphics appears later in this chapter.

GRAPHICS

Visual Logic graphics are a variation on **Logo Programming Language**, which has been used in educational settings for over three decades. The graphics commands are based on the idea that a pen can be instructed to move over a drawing board, leaving a mark as it moves. The drawing board is illustrated in Figure 6-1. Note that the coordinates (0, 0) are at the center of the screen and that north, east, south, and west are 0 degrees, 90 degrees, 180 degrees, and 270 degrees respectively. These are absolute positions and directions that do not change.

The 14 graphics commands available in the Visual Logic system can be accessed through the Element menu, as shown in Figure 6-2. Each command is described in Table 6-1. These graphics commands can be combined with other Visual Logic commands to create many interesting programs, as we will see shortly.

FORWARD AND TURN RIGHT

The first two graphics commands we examine are **Forward** and **Turn Right**. The Forward command moves the pen a specified number of units. If the pen is down, a line is drawn. If the pen is up, it moves without making a mark. The Turn Right command rotates the drawing direction a specified number of degrees. The pen does not move and does not make any marks.

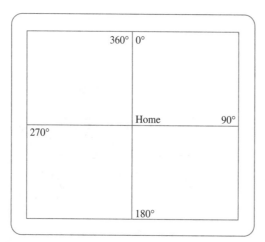

Figure 6-1 Absolute graphics positions

Figure 6-2 Visual Logic graphics commands

Command	Description
Forward **N**	Move the turtle N units forward (in the current direction)
Back **N**	Move the turtle N units backward (opposite the current direction)
Turn Right **D**	Turn the turtle D degrees to the right (clockwise)
Turn Left **D**	Turn the turtle D degrees to the left (counterclockwise)
Move to **X, Y**	Move the turtle to specified X, Y screen position
Go Home	Move the turtle to the center of the screen, facing up (north)
Set Color **C**	Set the pen color to the specific color C
Color Forward **F**	Step through a fixed color palette by F
Pen Width **N**	Set the pen width to N units
Circle **N**	Draw a circle with a center at the current location and a radius of N units
Fill Circle **N**	Draw a circle with a center at the current location and a radius of N units; fill the circle using the current pen color
Pen Up	Lift the turtle pen so that no lines are drawn as the turtle moves
Pen Down	Lower the turtle pen so that a line is drawn as the turtle moves
Set Direction **D**	Rotate the turtle so it faces D degree

Table 6-1 Descriptions of Turtle Graphic Commands

Consider the graphics program shown in Figure 6-3a. By default, the pen begins at the home position, which is at the center of the screen facing north (the top of the screen). The first graphics command is Forward 100, which results in a line 100 units long drawn north, the initial drawing direction. The second command, Turn Right 90, turns the drawing direction right by 90 degrees. There is no movement, but its direction is now due east. The final command, Forward 50, causes the pen to move forward (in this case, east) 50 units. The exact length of the units will vary from screen to screen, but the second line should be half as long as the first line. The output is shown in Figure 6-3b.

Many interesting designs can be made using only the Forward and Turn Right commands. A program that draws a small square (sides 50 units in length) is shown in Figure 6-4a. Figure 6-4b shows the step-by-step actions of the turtle when following the commands. A small turtle icon has been included in the images to illustrate the drawing direction at each stage. Note that the last command, Turn Right 90, is not necessary for drawing the square. However, it does return the drawing direction to exactly where it started. This can be helpful when drawing multiple figures.

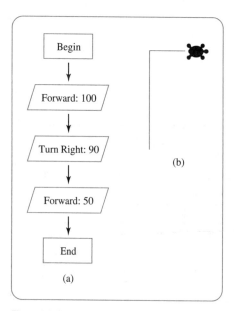

Figure 6-3 A graphics right angle

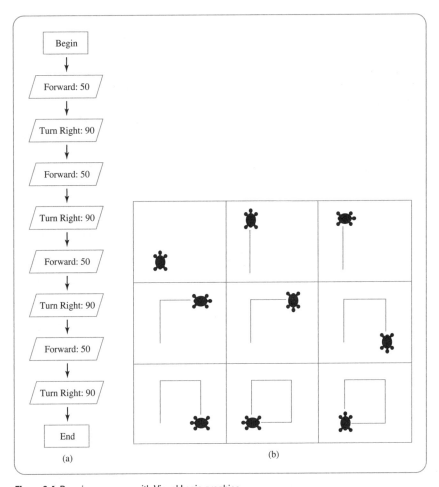

>> TIP
The commands Turn Right and Turn Left do not move the pen. They only rotate the drawing direction.

(a)

(b)

Figure 6-4 Drawing a square with Visual Logic graphics

QUICK CHECK 6-A

Using only Forward and Turn Right commands, draw the shapes in Figure 6-5. (*Hint*: The drawing must rotate a total of 360 degrees to return to its original direction.)

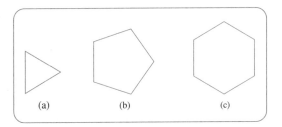

(a)   (b)   (c)

Figure 6-5 Forward and Turn Right Quick Check problem

USING LOOPS

At this point you should have successfully drawn the four shapes (triangle, square, pentagon, and hexagon) from the previous section. In doing so, you probably noticed a couple of patterns about the shape-drawing process. The first pattern is the repetition of the commands Forward and Turn Right. These two commands appear the same number of times as the sides of the figure. The second pattern is not so obvious.

The degrees the drawing direction must turn right are different for each shape and are based on the number of sides in the shape. Since the drawing direction will end up facing the same direction it started, the sum of all the right turns should be 360 degrees. The drawing direction should therefore rotate right 360 / N degrees after every turn, where N is the number of sides on the figure.

Determining patterns can make it easier to write programs because a pattern can be expressed once and repeated many times with a loop. The program shown in Figure 6-6a illustrates how a loop can be used to make a shape-drawing solution. The user enters the number of sides desired for the shape, and then a loop is used to draw the sides of the shapes. Inputs of 3, 5, and 6 would draw the shapes shown in Figure 6-5. An input of 10 would generate a decagon (10 sides), as shown in Figure 6-6b.

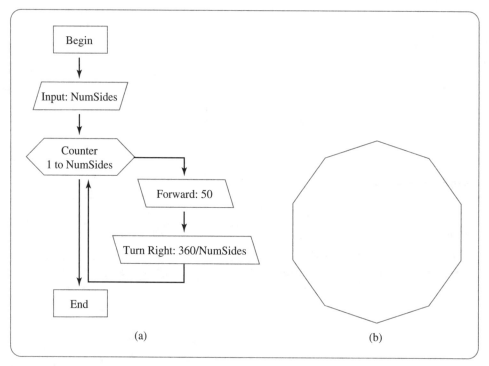

(a)   (b)

Figure 6-6 A shape-drawing program with a sample decagon output

When the loop variable is included inside the body of the loop, the output can be interesting. For example, Figure 6-7 creates a spiral by drawing increasingly longer lines after each turn. Figure 6-8 shows the same program with a 91-degree rotation.

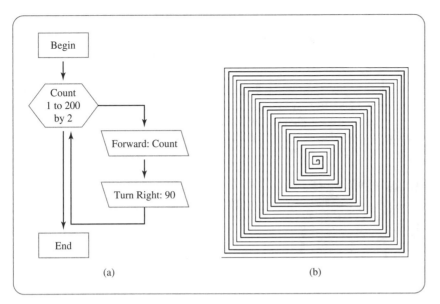

Figure 6-7 A spiral program and output

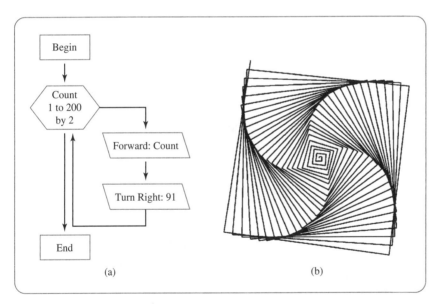

Figure 6-8 A spiral program with a 91-degree rotation

WORKING WITH COLORS

By default, the pen draws with black ink and is 1 unit in width. Visual Logic provides commands for changing the pen's color and width. The ability to manipulate the pen gives developers even greater opportunity to be creative in their designs.

SET COLOR AND PEN WIDTH

The **Set Color** command allows the developer to select any color from the standard Color dialog box. Figure 6-9 shows the Color dialog with custom colors expanded. The **Pen Width** command changes the thickness of the drawing pen.

A yellow circle and a series of thick yellow lines combine to look like a sun as shown in Figure 6-10. Notice that when the pen color is changed to yellow, it stays yellow for the rest of the program (or at least until it is changed again later). *Note*: When you select a Pen Color from the color pallet, the flowchart will give the RGB color breakdown. Thus, when you select Yellow, it appears as (255, 255, 0).

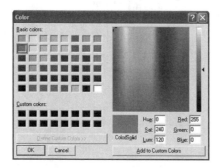

Figure 6-9 The Color dialog box (expanded)

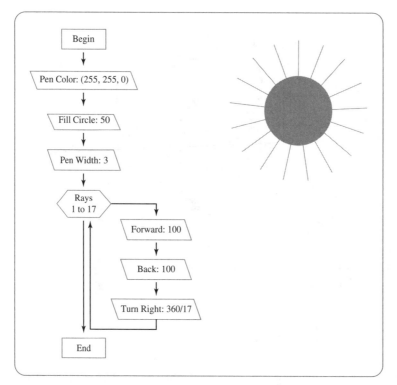

Figure 6-10 Sun algorithm and output

COLOR FORWARD

Another way of changing the pen color is to use the **Color Forward** command. This command moves the pen through the three base colors of red, green, and blue. There are 256 color variations between blue and green, 256 color variations between green and red, and 256 color variations between red and blue, at which point the color cycle begins again. The Color Forward command typically occurs inside a loop.

Figure 6-11 shows one use of the Color Forward command. The program draws increasingly larger circles with the pen color rotating through shades of blue, green, and red. If the default pen width of 1 is used, some pixels are left uncolored because of mathematical rounding. The slightly thicker pen width of 2 makes the colors solid between the concentric circles.

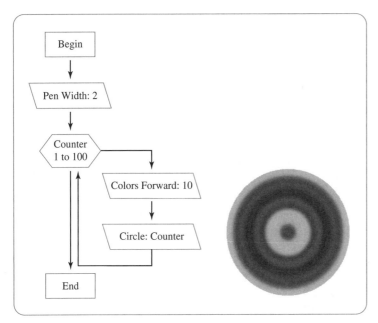

Figure 6-11 Colored concentric circles program and output

QUICK CHECK 6-B

Modify the solution in Figure 6-11 in the following ways and see how the image changes.

1. Change the Color Forward value to 5.

2. Change the Color Forward value to 256.

3. Change the Color Forward back to 10, then set the pen width to the default value 1. Notice how small mathematical rounding errors affect the image with this smaller pen size.

STRUCTURED DESIGN USING PROCEDURES

As problems become larger and more complicated, it becomes necessary to design solutions in a systematic manner. One common approach is called **structured design**. When structured design is used, a problem is broken into smaller pieces, each of which is solved individually. The solution to an individual piece of the problem is often stored in a procedure.

A **procedure** is a series of instructions that are grouped together and treated as a single unit. The procedure can be called from elsewhere in the solution by referencing the procedure's name. When the procedure is called, control flows to the statements inside the procedure. When the procedure is finished, control returns to the calling statement (Figure 6-12).

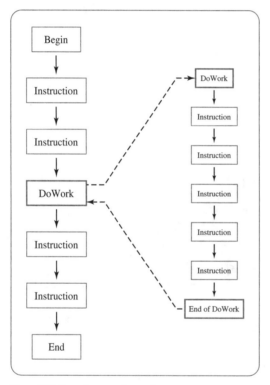

Figure 6-12 Flow of a procedure call

ROTATING FLAGS PROBLEM

To understand how procedures are created and used, consider the problem of drawing eight rotating flags. There is no single command for drawing a flag, but if there was such a command, the solution to this problem would probably look like Figure 6-13.

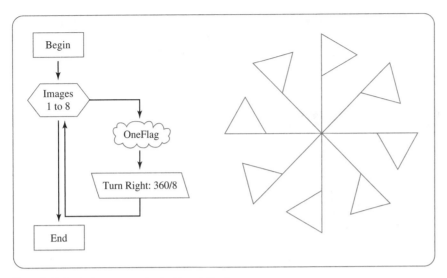

Figure 6-13 Desired program and output for rotating flags

>>**TIP** Procedures allow programs to be divided into logical units. For example, Figure 6-13 shows how the Rotating Flags program would work if "OneFlag" were a single command. Creating a "OneFlag" procedure will give the user a single command to perform all the work necessary to draw a single flag, thus making the flowchart in Figure 6-13 a valid solution.

The flowchart in Figure 6-13 represents the highest level of our structured design. The details of how a flag is drawn are not important at this level. When considering the solution at this highest level, it is assumed the OneFlag procedure will do what it is supposed to do (e.g., draw one flag).

CREATING A PROCEDURE

To create a procedure in Visual Logic, select "Procedures | Add New Procedure" from the main menu (Figure 6-14).

Figure 6-14 Menu option to add new procedure

The Procedure Edit dialog box appears, containing a text box for the name of the procedure and a list box for the parameters. (Parameters allow communication between the procedure and the calling program. Parameters are discussed later in this chapter.) Enter **OneFlag** into the text box (Figure 6-15) and press OK.

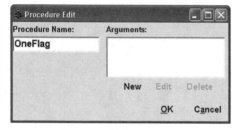

Figure 6-15 The Procedure Edit dialog box

After you press OK, Visual Logic creates an empty procedure stub with the name you specified (Figure 6-16).

Figure 6-16 The OneFlag procedure stub

Commands are added to the procedure exactly the same as they are in the main routine. Drawing the flag begins by drawing the pole (70 units long) on which the flag flies. The flag itself is a triangle with sides of 50 units. After the triangle is drawn, the procedure moves the pen back to the initial starting location. The full implementation of the OneFlag procedure is shown in Figure 6-17.

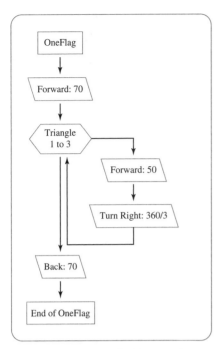

Figure 6-17 The complete OneFlag procedure

The OneFlag procedure is now finished. Return to the main procedure by selecting from the main menu "Procedures | Main." You may use the Call Procedure submenu as shown in Figure 6-18 to create a call to the OneFlag procedure. Use the OneFlag procedure to implement the Main level solution shown in Figure 6-19. The output for this program matches the desired output originally presented in Figure 6-13.

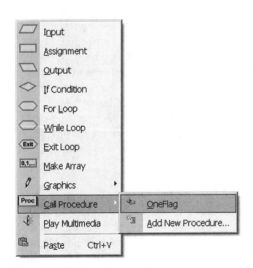

Figure 6-18 Calling a flag procedure

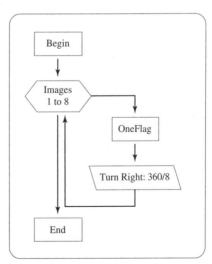

Figure 6-19 The solution for the rotating flags problem

QUICK CHECK 6-C

Using the OneFlag procedure, write programs that generate the output shown in Figure 6-20.

Figure 6-20 Output for two different programs, each utilizing the OneFlag procedure

PROCEDURES WITH PARAMETERS

Consider again the OneFlag procedure from the previous section. Whenever that procedure is called, the result is always the same, drawing a single flag shape. Procedures can be more flexible than this. For example, a procedure could be written that draws a multisided shape, and the number of sides could change from drawing to drawing. To do this, we would need to call the procedure and also provide additional information, for example the number of sides the shape should have. This can be done using parameters. A parameter is a piece of information that is communicated between the calling code and the procedure. The parameter is referred to as an **actual parameter** when calling the procedure and as a **formal parameter** inside the procedure body. To illustrate using a procedure with a parameter, consider the following rotating shapes program.

ROTATING SHAPES PROGRAM

If there was a procedure that would draw an AnySided figure (where the number of sides in the figure to be drawn is specified when calling the procedure) then the flowchart in Figure 6-21 would be able to produce the outputs shown in the bottom of the figure. The first output shows three rotations of a six-sided figure. The second output shows six rotations of a six-sided figure. (*Note*: The second output looks like a stack of blocks, but it is actually six hexagons.) Finally, the third output in Figure 6-21 is the result of rotating 10 pentagons.

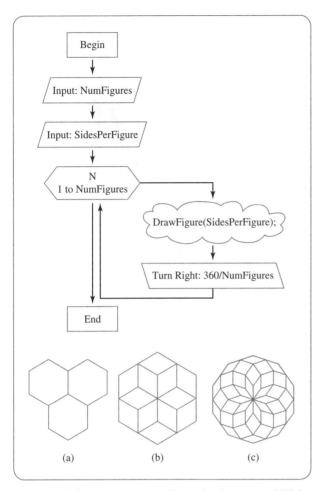

Figure 6-21 Various outputs generated by rotating shapes around 360 degrees

VISUAL LOGIC IMPLEMENTATION

Now consider the challenge of implementing the high-level solution design shown in Figure 6-21. We begin by implementing the conceptual action DrawFigure(NumSides) as a procedure. Select Add New Procedure from the Procedures menu. In the Procedure Edit dialog box, give the procedure the name **DrawFigure**. Then click the New button under the Arguments (or Parameters) box, and name the formal parameter **NumSides** (Figure 6-22a). Press OK to accept the new argument and your Procedure Edit dialog will look like Figure 6-22b. Press OK to close the Edit dialog window.

> **» TIP**
> Parameters are also known as *"arguments,"* which is the term used in the Procedure Edit dialog box.

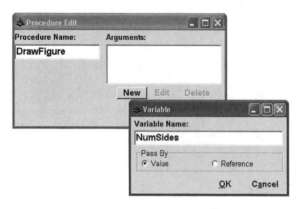
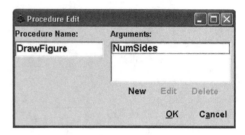

(a) Click "New" and enter argument   (b) New argument appears in Arguments list

Figure 6-22 Creating a procedure argument

Notice that the DrawFigure header and footer elements include the formal argument NumSides in parentheses. In most high-level programming languages, the parameters appear inside of parentheses after the procedure name.

Write the body of the procedure as follows. First add a For loop that iterates from 1 to the value of the formal argument **NumSides**. The body of the loop should draw one side of the image and rotate an appropriate amount so that the entire figure covers 360 degrees. Figure 6-23 shows the completed DrawFigure procedure.

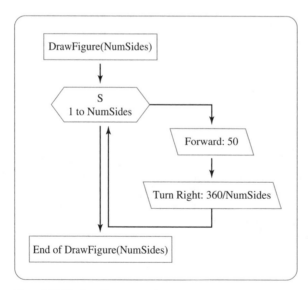

Figure 6-23 The DrawFigure procedure

112

The DrawFigure procedure is now finished. Return to the main procedure, where you should implement the high-level solution design shown in Figure 6-21. After you add the procedure call for DrawFigure, you should double-click on the procedure call to open the Arguments dialog box. Notice that you cannot edit either the procedure name ("DrawFigure") or the formal argument name ("NumSides") from this window. However, you can (and should!) edit the actual argument value that appears to the right of the formal argument. Enter **SidesPerFigure** as the actual argument as shown in Figure 6-24. (Remember that the actual argument is a variable or expression provided when calling the procedure, and the actual argument value is copied as the initial value for the formal argument during the current pass through the procedure code. In this case, the user's input value SidesPerFigure is passed to the procedure to become the initial value for the NumSides parameter.)

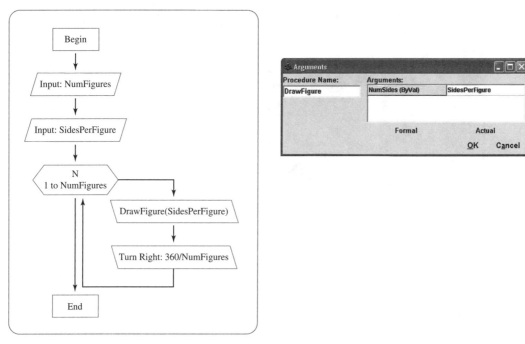

Figure 6-24 Rotating shapes solution with SidesPerFigure as an actual argument

When Figure 6-23 and Figure 6-24 are complete as shown, you can test the program by running it three times. The input pairs of {**3, 6**}, {**6, 6**}, and {**10, 10**} should generate the three outputs shown in Figure 6-21. Continue running the program using different input values, and see what kind of interesting drawings you can create.

PROCEDURES WITH PARAMETERS SUMMARY
» A parameter is a means of sharing information between the calling program and a procedure.
» Formal parameters are declared in the Procedure Edit dialog box at the same time as the procedure name. Formal parameters are displayed in parentheses after the procedure name in the procedure's header and footer elements.

» The calling program specifies the actual parameters at the time of the procedure call. Actual parameters are displayed in parentheses after the procedure name in the procedure call element.

RECURSION

The rotating shapes solution from the previous section involved a procedure with a single parameter. Procedures can contain as many parameters as necessary to pass all the desired information between the calling program and the procedure. To illustrate the use of multiple parameters, start a new application and create a procedure named **BentLine**. Under the Arguments list box, click the New button to add the parameter **Size**, and click OK. Then click the New button again to add a second parameter **Count** and then click OK. Your Procedure Edit dialog box should have two arguments, Size and Count, as shown in Figure 6-25.

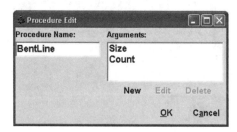

Figure 6-25 BentLine procedure declaration with two arguments

Close the Procedure Edit dialog box. Visual Logic creates a procedure stub for BentLine containing the two parameters Size and Count in the parameter list. Add the code for the BentLine procedure as shown in Figure 6-26, including the formal versus actual values that you should specify when editing (double-clicking) the Call Procedure flowchart elements.

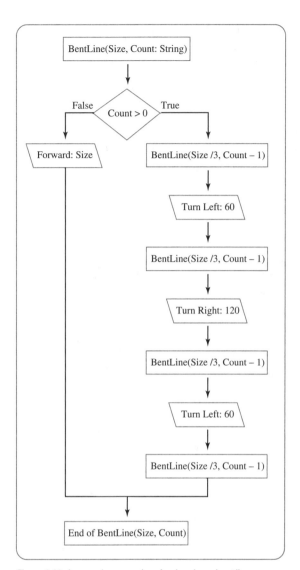
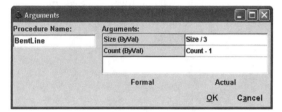

Figure 6-26 A recursive procedure for drawing a bent line

Notice that inside the BentLine procedure there is a call to the BentLine procedure itself. (Actually, there are four calls to itself inside the procedure.) BentLine is therefore a **recursive procedure**, meaning it is a procedure that calls itself. A recursive procedure is similar to a loop in that the code inside the procedure will be repeated many times. You must be cautious when writing recursive procedures to avoid infinite recursion. A recursive procedure therefore typically begins by performing a test on one of its parameters to check for a base case. If the base case is satisfied, then the procedure does not call itself. If the base case is not satisfied, then the procedure does some processing that includes a recursive call. In Figure 6-26, the base case test is Count > 0. If the test is True, then the procedure recursively calls itself and draws a smaller (e.g., Size / 3) line with a lower (e.g., Count − 1) base value. Eventually, the value for Count will be zero, at which time the procedure will simply draw a line of length Size without making a recursive call. (This is how the procedure avoids an infinite loop.)

After writing the BentLine procedure, return to the main procedure and add a call to BentLine. Double-click on the procedure element and enter actual parameter values of 200 and 1 to the formal parameters of Size and Count respectively.

When you close the Parameters dialog box, the main program will look like Figure 6-27.

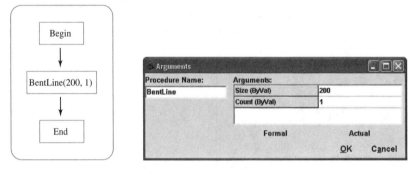

Figure 6-27 The main body with a call to the recursive BentLine procedure

Run the solution. You should get a line with a single bend. Edit the Count parameter to 2 and rerun the solution. Then change the Count value to 3 and 4, running the solution after each change. You should generate outputs similar to Figure 6-28.

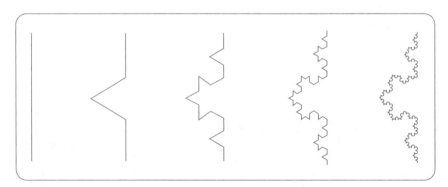

Figure 6-28 BentLine output results for runs with Count being 0, 1, 2, 3, and 4

»CASE STUDY SOLUTION

Drawing Houses

Problem: Write a program to generate a series of houses similar to the image shown in Figure 6-29.

Analysis: The image contains 45 houses, each drawn using a random pen color. The design for each house is the same: a square base with a triangle roof and two windows. The final figure will contain 45 houses and 90 windows. To help handle the complexity and to avoid repeating code, procedures are used.

The **DrawWindow** procedure (Figure 6-30) draws a window as four contiguous squares. The position of the window is specified by the arguments passed to the procedure.

The **DrawHouse** procedure (Figure 6-31) draws the house as a square frame under a triangle roof. The position of the house is specified by the arguments passed to the procedure. Additionally, the DrawHouse procedure calls the DrawWindow procedure twice to add the two windows at the proper position.

The high-level solution for this problem (Figure 6-32) specifies the maximum house size and, based on that value, determines the yard size for each house (so the houses do not overlap with each other.) The high-level solution then draws the 45 houses at different horizontal and vertical positions on the screen based on changing X and Y values. Each house has a random size and a random color, and the drawing of the house is done by calling the DrawHouse procedure.

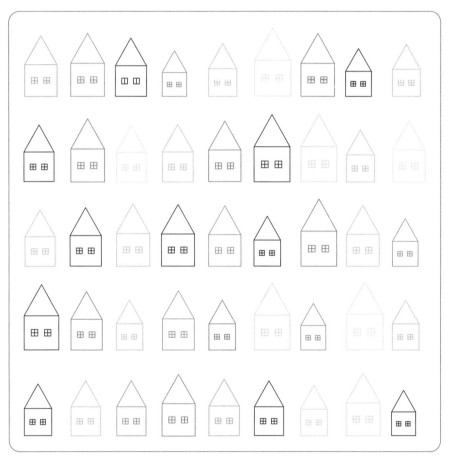

Figure 6-29 Houses output

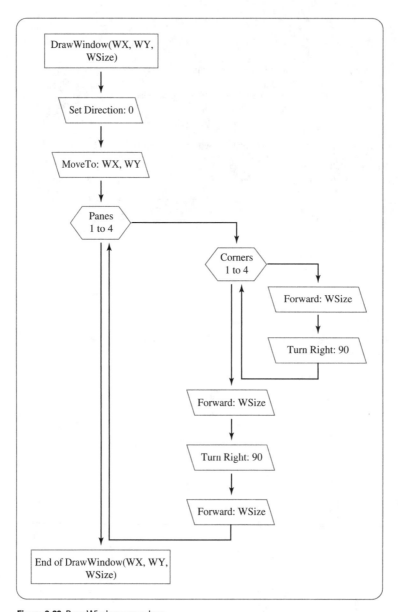

Figure 6-30 DrawWindow procedure

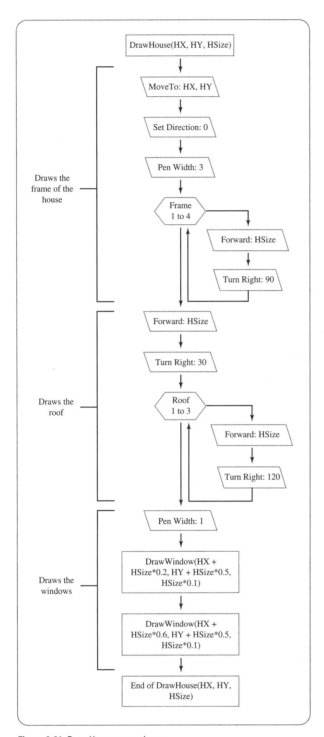

Figure 6-31 DrawHouse procedure

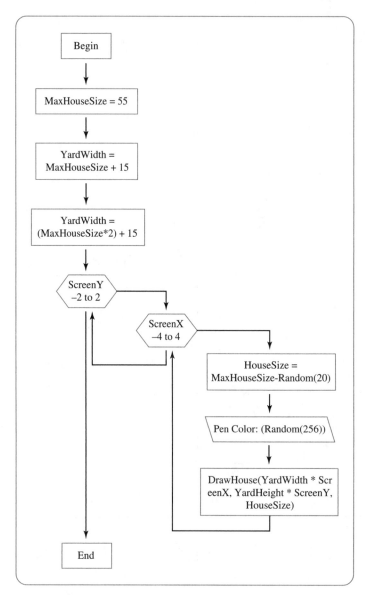

Figure 6-32 High-level solution to draw house problem

CHAPTER SUMMARY

» Visual Logic graphics include commands, such as Forward and Right. These commands move a virtual pen across the screen.

» Procedures allow code to be written once and called many times. Procedures also allow for code to be organized by logical function.

» An actual parameter is a value or reference passed from the calling code to a procedure. A formal parameter is the corresponding variable in the procedure that receives the value or reference.

KEY TERMS

actual parameter	Logo Programming Language	recursive procedure
Color Forward	parameter	Set Color
formal parameter	Pen Width	structured design
Forward	procedure	Turn Right

REVIEW QUESTIONS

1. What is the Visual Logic graphics pen, and how is it related to the Logo Programming Language turtle?

2. If the current pen drawing direction is north and you want to draw a line from the current position to a point 100 units to the east, what graphics command(s) would you use?

3. Explain the difference between the Set Color command and the Color Forward command.

4. Explain the difference between the Circle command and the Fill Circle command.

5. What is structured design? How does it benefit developers when solving large problems?

6. What is a procedure? What happens when a procedure is called? What happens when a procedure is finished executing?

7. What is the purpose of a parameter? What is the difference between a formal parameter and an actual parameter?

8. What is a recursive procedure? How does a recursive procedure avoid infinite recursion?

PROGRAMMING EXERCISES

6-1. Raising Flags. Draw four flags of increasing sizes.

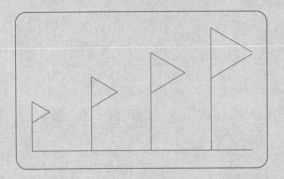

6-2. Rotating Rectangles. Write a graphics program with three inputs: rectangle height, rectangle width, and number of rectangles. The program should then display the specified rectangles rotated around a center point. Two sample runs are shown below. In the first output shown, the input values were 100, 50, 5. In the second sample run shown below, the input values were 50, 200, 7. (Only one set of rotating rectangles should appear each time you run the program, and the shape and number of rectangles will depend on the three input values.)

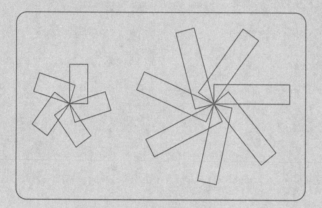

6-3. Concentric Squares. Use the Color Forward command to generate a series of concentric squares similar to the following figure.

6-4. CD Burn. It is always a good idea to back up your files on a regular basis, and this process has been made easier by affordable CD burners. Generate an image similar to the following to remind others that frequently backing up your hard drive on CD is a good idea. (*Hint*: This can be drawn similar to sun rays in Figure 6-10 only with color changes.)

6-5. Random Flags. Write a program that uses a flag-drawing procedure to draw 10 flags at random locations. Every time you run the program, the flags should show up at different locations on the screen. Therefore, the position of your 10 flags will be different than those shown in the figure below.

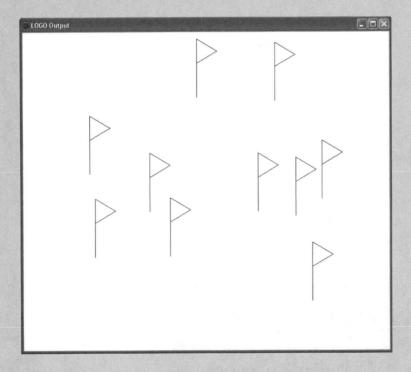

6-6. Random Other. Write a program with a procedure that draws a shape of your choice. (In the example below, the shape is a stickman figure.) Your program should then call the procedure 10 times to draw the shape at 10 random locations. Every time you run the program, your shape should show up at different locations on the screen. Therefore, the position of your 10 shapes will be different than those shown in the figure below.

6-7. Fireworks. Consider the image of fireworks in a nighttime sky. Write a procedure called Burst that moves the pen to a random location on the screen, moves the pen color forward 256, and then draws a firework burst with a random size and number of rays. (*Hint*: You may want to add a minimum value to the random size and random number of rays to avoid having bursts that are too small or have too few rays.) The main procedure should call Burst multiple times to generate an image similar to the image below. *Note*: Because of the random values, your solution image will be different each time you run your program. (*Hint*: You can create a nighttime background by setting the pen color to black and then calling Fill Circle with a sufficiently large value, such as 2000.)

VISUAL LOGIC
RESERVED WORDS

The following are reserved words that Visual Logic uses for special purposes and therefore these cannot (or should not) be used as variable or procedure names.

And	Except	Not	Shr
Array	File	Object	String
As	Finally	Of	Then
Begin	For	On	ThreadVar
Case	Function	Or	To
Class	Goto	Packed	Try
Const	If	Procedure	Type
Constructor	Implementation	Program	Unit
Destructor	In	Property	Until
Div	Inherited	Raise	Uses
Do	Interface	Record	Var
DownTo	Is	Repeat	While
Else	Length	Set	With
End	Mod	Shl	Xor

B

DEBUGGING IN VISUAL LOGIC

Eventually, all developers write programs that contain errors. This appendix contains some suggestions on how to identify and fix errors in your program.

COMMON MISTAKE #1: CHECK FOR MISSPELLED VARIABLE NAMES

One of the most common errors that novice students will make is mistyping their variable names. For example, if you input "Height" and then later perform a calculation "Area = Width * Heigth", your Area value will be zero (0). This is because "Height" and "Heigth" are different variable names. The first holds the input value and the second is a different, unassigned variable and therefore has the default value of zero. So the assignment statement is basically "Area = Width * 0" which gives the zero result.

Strangely enough, consistent spelling is more important than correct spelling. If you misspell "Heigth" in both instances above, the program will work. Of course, correct and consistent spelling is best!

COMMON MISTAKE #2: MULTIPLE VARIABLE NAMES

This is similar to the first common mistake, but rather than having a typing error, your program might have two different variables for the same value. Consider two inputs for "Height" and "Width", then the assignment "Area = Height * Size". This would also produce a zero (0) result because the input value "Width" is not used in the calculation, but instead an unassigned new variable "Size" is used. Other example would be to use both "Max" and "Maximum" when referencing the same value.

The thing to remember here is to pick one descriptive variable name and stick with it.

DEBUGGING—PENCIL AND PAPER

If the common mistakes above did not solve your problem, you will need to examine your solution logic more closely. A pencil and paper remains one of the most powerful tools of engineers and inventors, which is good because programming involves a little of both. A "desk check" is a manual (pencil and paper) technique for checking the logic of an algorithm. Your goal is to carefully mimic exactly what the computer will do when executing the program, writing down each variable name and how the values for each variable changes while the program executes. When the variable's values change, simply cross out the old values and write down the new values below the variable name. By stepping through the entire program this way you are likely to determine why your program is not working, and hopefully it will be clear what needs to change to fix the problem.

DEBUGGING—BREAKPOINTS AND VARIABLE WATCH

Finally, if you still cannot figure out why your program is not working, you can try debugging your program by stepping through your program one element at a time. The main menu contains a "Debug" menu option with six options. The "Step Into" option will cause a Variable Watch window to appear and will move through your program one element at a time. (*Note:* You can also hit the F8 key as a shortcut for "Step Into".) When running your program like this you are said to be in Debug mode and you can monitor how the variable values change as you step through the solution.

Note that the current flowchart element is highlighted by a flashing background. Also note that an Input dialog box might appear in the background when running in debug mode (so that you have to click on the item in the Taskbar at the bottom of the screen.) Finally, when doing input, be sure to click in the input window text box so that your input value appears in the proper window.

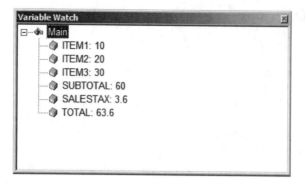

By examining the program variables and watching their values change as each step of the program executes, hopefully you will better understand what is happening when your program runs, and therefore be better able to fix any problems that exist.

C

USING MULTIMEDIA

One feature of Visual Logic that is not directly covered in this Guide is the last menu element "Play Multimedia". This is an optional element that can be introduced in the first chapter, or can be ignored for the entire book. However it is very easy to use and is something that can dramatically change the look and feel of your solutions.

Visual Logic can support .wav audio and .mp3 video formats, and may support other formats as well depending on the encoding used. By placing the "Play Multimedia" element in the proper, logical location you can give the use a richer audio-video experience when running your solution.

The possibilities are limited only by your imagination. Have fun being creative!

INDEX

Special Characters
\- (back slash), 11
> (greater than operator), 21
> (less than operator), 21
( ) (parentheses), 26
<> (not equal operator), 21
" (quotation mark), 6
§ (console end-of-output symbol), 38–39
& (ampersand), 6
* (asterisk), 8, 11
+ (plus sign), 8, 11
− (minus sign), 8, 11
/ (slash), 8, 11
>= (greater than or equal operator), 21
<= (less than or equal operator), 21
^ (caret), 11
= equal sign, 21

A

accumulator, 47, 48, 49
actual parameter, 110
addition operator (+), 8, 11
algorithm, 2–3
ampersand (&), concatenation
    operator, 6
AND operator, 26
argument. *See* parameter
arithmetic expression, 11–13
array, 73–91
    accessing individual elements, 74–75
    benefits of using, 75–78
    creating, 74
    dice roll simulation program, 81–83
    elements, 74
    evens and odds program, 78–80
    index, 74, 75, 78
    For loop, 78
    parallel arrays program, 83–90
    sorting, 87–89
    upper bound, 74
assignment statement, 8–9
asterisk (*), multiplication operator,
    8, 11

B

back slash (, integer division operator, 11
bubble sort, 87–89
bug, 14

C

caret (^), exponentiation operator, 11
color, graphics, 103–105
Color dialog box, 104
Color Forward command, 105
command. *See also specific commands*
    sequential, 20
compound condition, 25–27, 28, 30, 31
computer program, 1
concatenation operator, 6
condition, 20
    nested, 28, 29
console end-of-output symbol (§),
    38–39
console input, 37–38
console output, 37–39
conversion, units of measurement, 12–13
counter, 47, 48, 49
counting backwards program, 43–44

D

debugging, 14
decision making, 19–33
    compound conditions, 25–27, 28,
        30, 31
    computer capability, 20
    IF statement, 20–23
    nested IF statements, 23–25
determine the average program, 47–48
dice roll simulation program, 81–83
Dijkstra, Edward, 20
division, 11
division operator (/), 8, 11
double quote ("), string literals, 6
drawing houses program, 117–120

E

Edison, Thomas, 14
element, array, 74
  accessing, 74–75
  index, 74, 75, 78
  referencing, 75
end-of-output symbol (§), 38–39
equal operator (=), 21
equal sign (=), equal operator, 21
evens and odds program, 78–80
Exit loop, 49–52
  high-low game program, 51–52
exponentiation, 11
exponentiation operator (ˆ), 11
expression, 8

F

final value, For loop, 59, 61–63
flowchart, 3–5
  without execution, 5
Flowchart Elements menu, 3–4
For loop, 59–63
  arrays, 78
  final value, 59, 61–63
  initial value, 59, 61
  step value, 59, 61–63
  While loops compared, 60–61
formal parameter, 110
format
  programming, 6–7
  username and password storage, 84
Forward command, 98–101
function, intrinsic, 13–14

G

graphics, 98–103
  colors, 103–105
  commands, 98, 99
  Forward command, 98–101
  loops, 102–103
  Turn Left command, 101
  Turn Right command, 98–101
greater than operator (>), 21
greater than or equal operator (>=), 21

H

Hello Name program, 5–7
Hello World program, 3–5
high-low game program, 51–52
Hopper, Grace Mary, 14

I

IF statement, 20–23
  nested, 23–25
index, array elements, 74, 75, 78

infinite loop, 42
initial value, For loop, 59, 61
input
  console, 37–38
  weekly paycheck program, 7–8
input statement, 5
integer division, 11
integer division operator (, 11
integer remainder, 11
intrinsic function, 13–14

L

less than operator (>), 21
less than or equal operator (<=), 21
Logo Programming Language, 98
loop
  Exit loop, 49–52
  graphics, 102–103
  infinite, 42
  For loop. See For loop
  nested. See nested loop
  While. See While loop
Loop Control Variable, 40

M

Make Array command, 74
measurement units, conversion, 12–13
minus sign (−), subtraction operator, 8, 11
multiplication, 11
multiplication operator (*), 8, 11
multiplication table program, 65–67

N

nested condition, 28, 29
nested IF statement, 23–25
nested loop, 63–68
  multiplication table program, 65–67
  triangle problem program, 67–68
not equal operator (<>), 21
NOT operator, 26
numeric input, 6

O

OR operator, 26
output
  console, 37–39
  format for statements, 9, 11
  forms, 9, 11
  weekly paycheck program, 9–11

P

Papert, Semore, 98
parallel arrays program, 83–90
parameter, 110–114
  actual, 110

parameter (*continued*)
    formal, 110
    rotating shapes program, 110–111
    Visual Logic implementation, 111–113
parentheses (()), compound conditions, 26
password, parallel arrays program, 83–90
Pen Width command, 104
placeholder variable, 28, 32
plus sign (+), addition operator, 8, 11
post-test loop, 43
pre-test loop, 43
procedure, 106. *See also* structured design
    using procedures
    calling, 109
    creating, 107–109
    names, 108
    parameters, 110–114
    recursive, 114–116
processing, weekly paycheck program, 8–9
program, 1
programming format, 6–7

Q

quotation mark ("), string literals, 6

R

random integer, 81
reading data from a text file, 83–84
recursive procedure, 114–116
relational operator, 20–21
repetition, 20
rotating flags program, 106–107
rotating shapes program, 110–111

S

selection, 20
sentinel value, 46–49
    determine the average program, 47–48
sequential command, 20
Set Color command, 104
signaling value, 46–49
slash (/), division operator, 8, 11
sorting an array, 87–89
step value, For loop, 59, 61–63
string literal, 6
structured design using procedures, 106–109
    creating procedures, 107–109
    procedures with parameters, 110–114

recursion, 114–116
    rotating flags program, 106–107
    rotating shapes program, 110–111
    Visual Logic implementation, 111–113
"Structured Programming" (Dijkstra), 20
subtraction operator (−), 8, 11
syntax, 3

T

text file, reading data, 83–84
triangle problem program, 67–68
Turn Left command, 101
Turn Right command, 98–101

U

units of measurement, conversion, 12–13
upper bound, 74
username, parallel arrays program, 83–90

V

value
    final, 59, 61–63
    initial, 59, 61
    sentinel (signaling), 46–49
    step, 59, 61–63
variable, 5
    Loop Control Variable, 40
    placeholder, 28, 32
Visual Logic, 2

W

weekly paycheck program, 7–11
    input, 7–8
    output, 9–11
    processing, 8–9
While loop, 40–49
    counting backwards program, 43–44
    Exit loops with, 49, 50
    For loops compared, 60–61
    post-test, 43
    pre-test, 43
    sentinel values, 46–49

X

XOR operator, 26